POLITICS OF AGING AMONG ELDER HISPANICS

Fernando M. Torres-Gil
University of Southern California

UNIVERSITY
PRESS OF
AMERICA

To my wife, Elvira;
my mother, Maria de Jesus; and
my grandmother, Andrea Arredondo de Raya.

Acknowledgements

This book could not have been accomplished without the support and assistance of many persons. Several professors were early contributors to my education and my interest in political science, social policy and gerontology: Dr. Braverman, Mr. Newton and Mr. Mounkes from Hartnell College and Dr. Ballard and Dr. McCraw from San Jose State University. The study from where the initial data derived involved several individuals who will be long remembered: Ramona Sarinana, forever active with Hispanic seniors in San Jose; Phil Marquez, Father Moriarty, Father Roberts and Bertha Lopez who provided entry into the community; and my carnales from the area, especially the Viniegra family, who provided shelter and friendship.

The initial reason for the study, the completion of a dissertation, was accomplished at the Florence Heller Graduate School for Advanced Studies in Social Welfare at Brandeis University. The staff of the school--Nita, Millie, Ann, Maryann, Marsha, Barbara and Elaine--were caring and supportive. Several faculty members were instrumental in guiding and inspiring this work: Dr. Robert Binstock, who served as the dissertation chairman and to whom I owe much for the professional development he provided; Dr. Lawrence Fuchs, a source of inspiration and creativity: Dr. James Schulz, always available for advice and support; and Dr. Norman Kurtz, a friend and supporter. A fifth person, Dr. Rosina Becerra, was a friend and confidant who provided invaluable support.

The actual preparation of the book was accomplished with the tremendous support, assistance and encouragement of the Andrus Gerontology Center at the University of Southern California. Dr. James Birren and Dr. David Peterson, Dean and Director, respectively, of the Leonard Davis School of Gerontology, made the book possible by providing generous resources and support. The faculty of the Leonard Davis School of Gerontology were always ready with an encouraging word: Dr. Ruth Weg, Dr. Richard Davis, Dr. Steve Zarit, Dr. Mike Hendrickson, Dr. David Mangen and Dr. Nan Corby. The staff in particular was instrumental in providing the patience, cooperation, and assistance necessary for carrying out the assignments: Linda Oku, Kate Wilber, Pauline Abbott and Millie Allyn.

Various members of the Center provided many ideas, concepts and materials for the book: Neal Cutler,

Pauline Robinson, Warner Schaie, Ray Steinberg, Jon Pynoos and Bill Lammers. In particular, Vern Bengtson and Betty Hartford were invaluable in refining the concepts and themes presented in this book.

Other components of the Gerontology Center were helpful in the preparation of the manuscript: Jean Mueller, Stewart Greathouse and the staff from the Library and Dissemination Office; from the Computer Center: Marijo Walsh and Mary Jackson; Valerie Remnet, Vicki Plowman, Helen Dennis and Wayne Friedlander of the Educational Development Division; and Pauline Robinson, Deborah Newquist and Sally Coberly from the National Policy Center on Employment and Retirement. The students in my courses on Social Policy and Policies, Programs and Politics were very helpful in refining the details of the book.

Several individuals deserve a special debt of gratitude in the development of the book. Gail Doss, a friend, associate and staff assistant, was an invaluable asset who provided the solid support that allowed the project to bear fruition and who took special pride in its accomplishment. May Ng provided invaluable assistance in the preparation of the manuscript and went above and beyond the call of duty in the final preparation. Mimi Kmet provided valuable editing services.

Last but not least, the real mover in the project, my graduate assistant, Daisy Vanderupwich: without her this could not have been done. The countless hours, the late nights, and the willingness to assume overall coordination for the final preparation made this possible. Without her it would have been a vastly more difficult project.

In conclusion, I dedicate this book to the three women who matter most to me: Elvira, my wife; Maria de Jesus, my mother; and Andrea Arrendondo de Raya, my grandmother. My wife remained always faithful and patient, and my mother forever remains my motivation. My grandmother, in particular, was a source of inspiration in the politics of aging among elderly Hispanics and a model for living a long, happy, strong and productive life. She came to this country shortly after the Mexican Revolution as an immigrant seeking a better future; during the great depression and World War II, she struggled as a wife and mother to raise a family; and as a grandmother, she saw her extended family grow and prosper in this country. She is a model for the potential of elderly Hispanics in this country.

CONTENTS

TABLES

ILLUSTRATIONS

PREFACE

Although the political history of Hispanics includes a record of diverse political actions--union organizing, strikes, protests, voter registration drives--only within the last ten years have Hispanics acquired any meaningful political power. Hispanic political power has been manifested in the election of public officials including state governors, development of lobbying organizations, national advocacy organizations, and greater influence in public policy issues such as immigration, bilingual education and civil rights. The increase in political participation by Hispanics engendered by this new movement has served to dramatize the power and influence a politically aware and involved minority group can wield. Even though the Hispanic population continues to be one of the poorest and most excluded of all American minority groups, its increased political participation has been essential to any initial step taken towards social equality and economic security.

This increase in political participation, however, seems to be confined primarily to the young and middle-aged portions of the Hispanic population. Where does the elderly Hispanic fit into Hispanic politics? What is the role of the aged Latino in the various political activities that characterize Hispanic politics? Do they participate at all?

This book examines the extent and nature of political participation among elderly Mexican Americans. It specifically addresses the role of aged Mexican Americans within Hispanic related, age-related, and general electoral political processes, as well as an assessment of that population's attitudes toward various types of politics.

A random sample of 106 respondents--ages fifty-two to eighty-eight--was selected from San Jose, California. A questionnaire focusing on socioeconomic data, generational relations, ethnicity, political socialization, political attitudes and political participation was administered.

Additional data was gathered through an unstructured interview--with an assessment of personal experiences that affected political behavior --and from the 1980 Census.

The study and subsequent analysis of the data resulted in several significant findings. Although elderly Mexican Americans rated low in political participation, they rated high in political interest and awareness; many have been involved in political activities (e.g., strikes, labor union organizing) during their youth. Generational conflicts and ideological disagreement with Hispanic activists were not perceived as major problems, indicating potential for working with current Hispanic political groups. Political issues viewed most favorable by the respondents were Hispanic and age related politics. Major reasons cited for lack of political participation in Hispanic and age-related politics were a lack of communication (lack of information) and fear of negative consequences. The latter point stemmed, in part, from a tendency to defer to the political system rather than participate--a phenomenon rooted in the political culture of Mexico and negative political experiences (e.g., deportations, Mexican Revolution) in earlier life. United States birth and degree of acculturation were related to a high sense of efficacy and citizen duty, and high socioeconomic status and access to the political system correlated with political activity.

These findings suggest the potential for increased involvement by elderly Hispanics, indicating that greater communication between the young and the old may by an important resource for increasing the base of Hispanic political power. The 1980 Census reveals that the Hispanic population is increasing dramatically in size, and many references have been made to the "Decade of the Hispanic" during the 1980s. A little known fact in the 1980 data is that the elderly (those over sixty years old) is the fastest growing segment in the Hispanic population. Although Hispanics remain a basically young population they will age rapidly. That creates great potential for organizing Hispanics around ethnic issues and age related issues such as Social Security, Medicare, social services and age discrimination. At present, Hispanic elderly are not a subject of interest to scholars, politicians or Hispanic communities. However, this book indicates that they will amass the numbers and power to be heard, creating the potential for altering the political equation in Hispanic politics and aging issues in the United States.

This book serves as a first step in understanding

the dimensions and implications of this phenomena. Much more work will be needed. As the public, media, government and politicians take note of the increasingly important role of Hispanics and of senior citizens, they will take note of Hispanic elders and their role in the political process. It is vital that further work and research be conducted in this area. Social policy and public and private initiatives dealing with senior citizen programs and Hispanic issues will be affected by the role this group plays and the issues it pursues. In order to involve them in the democratic political processes of this country and in order to maximize their contributions it behooves us to understand the politics of aging among elderly Hispanics.

Fernando M. Torres-Gil
Los Angeles, California
July, 1982

CHAPTER I

POLITICS OF AGING AMONG ELDER HISPANICS

Introduction

The advent of Hispanic political power in the United States and increased political participation by Mexican-Americans, Cubans, Puerto Ricans and Latin Americans dramatize the power and influence a politically aware and involved minority group can wield. Although the political history of Hispanics--beginning with the United States' conquest of the Southwest in 1848 and the colonization of Puerto Rico and Cuba in the late nineteenth century--includes a record of such diverse political actions as union organizing, strikes, protests and voter registration drives, Hispanics have acquired visible political power only within the last fifteen years. Between 1965 and 1982 the United Farmworker's Union was formed, Hispanic student organizations have grown, a political third party (La Raza Unida) was created, and effective urban barrio organizations such as the United Neighborhood Organizations (UNO) and Communities Organized for Public Service (COPS) (Los Angeles and San Antonio, respectively) have appeared. The last fifteen years have witnessed the election of Hispanics to the Congress, state legislatures and the governorships in New Mexico and Arizona. This increased political participation is accomplishing concrete results in legislative initiatives, educational opportunities, reduction of electoral barriers and increased public awareness of Hispanic issues. Although Hispanics continue to be relatively poor and excluded as a minority population, their increased political participation is important in overcoming obstacles to the attainment of social equality and economic security.

However, social and economic improvements for elderly Hispanics-- los Ancianos-- do not seem to match improvements for Hispanics in general. For example, manpower training programs, veteran's benefits and affirmative action efforts, which are intended to improve the social and economic position of Hispanics, have generally benefited only the adult and the young; bilingual and bicultural curricula, designed to provide effective education, have generally assisted the young;

1

and legislation eliminating language requirements for voting has generally helped adult Hispanics to vote. But older Hispanics appear to have benefited less from those social and economic gains. Although senior citizen programs have been developed to provide nutrition, transportation, legal assistance and other services, older Hispanics have not benefited in proportion to their needs and numbers.

Perhaps Hispanic politics in recent years have not specifically encouraged the participation of older Hispanics. While Hispanic activists, researchers, professionals and politicians encourage other Hispanics to become more active politically and thus improve their social and economic conditions, they have tended to neglect elderly Hispanics. Most age groups and social classes in the Hispanic population identify with some form of political activism. For example, young Hispanics participate in a variety of high school and college political organizations; middle aged Hispanics maintain civic and political groups such as the League for United Latin American Citizens (LULAC), the GI Forum and the National Council of La Raza; barrio residents are represented in community action programs (The East Los Angeles Community Union); and rural Hispanics, comprised primarily of the middle aged and youth, are represented by rural community organizations and farmworker unions. Concurrently with the rise of Hispanic political power, "Senior Power" has developed in the United States. The "politics of aging" reflects the growing influence of older persons in this country through their increased numbers, sophisticated age-based organizations and increasing public attention to social policy issues of Medicare, Social Security, nursing home reform and age discrimination. As with Hispanic politics in general, too little attention has been paid to the role of elderly Hispanics in the politics of aging and to the extent that it intersects with Hispanic politics. Where does the elderly Hispanic fit into Hispanic politics? What is the role of elderly Hispanics in the various political activities that characterize Hispanic politics and senior citizen activities? Do they participate? Is it important that they represent themselves as a specific age and ethnic group, and if so, will they influence the strategies and directions Hispanic organizations currently follow?

Purpose

Answers to those questions are difficult to find, since research is very limited in the areas of Hispanic politics and the politics of aging. This book seeks to answer such questions through an exploration of the political attitudes and political participation of the Hispanic elderly. With some answers to those questions, Hispanics can increase their support to the elderly segments of that population through political activities and the elderly Hispanic may be encouraged to participate.¹

Inasmuch as we are concerned about the efficacy of Hispanic politics in improving the well being of older Hispanics, we should first gain some understanding of the extent and nature of that group's participation in Hispanic politics. As its immediate purpose, this inquiry will examine the extent and nature of such participation. Little is known about the political behavior of older Hispanics. This book proposes to examine the levels of political activity among them, their attitudes toward specific issues and the sources of variation in participation. This information can contribute to a greater understanding of the role of older Hispanics in Hispanic politics, in general citizenship, and in senior citizen activities; and a greater understanding can assist older Hispanics in improving their well being through politics.

The Hispanic population in the United States is noted for its diversity of linguistic dialects, culture, regional variations, and political interests. Cubans are greatly affected by the Cuban revolution of 1958 and are concentrated in Florida; Puerto Ricans maintain strong links with Puerto Rico and are found primarily on the East Coast and the "Island" of Puerto Rico; and Mexican-Americans interact regularly with Mexico and are concentrated in the Southwest and Midwest. In spite of this diversity, they also have much in common: relatively low social and economic conditions, minority status in the United States, desires for political and social equality, religion, customs, and language. This book uses as a case study the Mexican-American elderly in San Jose, California. To the extent that the commonalities mentioned above affect all subgroups of the Hispanic population, the findings uncovered from the San Jose subgroup will have applicability. Mexican-American elderly were chosen as the specific subgroup to investigate because of the

3

necessity for an in-depth examination of an elderly Hispanic group in a large urban area. The characteristics of San Jose as a large, urban metropolis with a high percentage of Hispanics are similar to many areas of the country with large concentrations of Hispanics; and the presence of Mexican-Americans, as well as Puerto Ricans and Cubans in the San Jose community reflects the cultural diversity of the Hispanic population.

This book will be an exploratory descriptive study. Exploratory descriptive inquiries generally formulate a problem for more precise investigation, develop hypotheses and describe a study population about which little is known (Sellitz et al., 1959). The present inquiry will be organized around tentative hypotheses, which will lay a foundation to which more definitive research can be added. At the same time the immediate reporting of the data will be confined to the context of the study population itself with supporting data and information utilized to provide generalizations for other subgroups of the Hispanic population.

Thus, the research task has been reduced to three relatively specific and encompassing objectives: 1) an examination of the levels of political activity among a sample of Hispanic elderly in California; 2) an assessment of the attitudes older Hispanics have toward Hispanic politics, general citizenship, and senior citizen affairs; 3) and an investigation of the sources of variation in the political participation of elderly Hispanics.

The first objective will provide basic information on actual participation among the study sample. With that data it will be possible to compare rates of political activity among elderly Hispanics with rates of activity among elderly Whites and with Hispanics in general. The second objective will describe the feelings and perceptions older Hispanics have about issues associated with Hispanic politics, general citizenship and senior activities. The third objective deals with the "why" and "why not" of political participation. The answers and findings will reveal trends in political behavior and the potential for political participation. The research assumes the study sample will demonstrate a variation in terms of political activity: some will participate more than others. Therefore, to investigate why some older

4

Hispanics are more active than others, the analysis will include an examination of the characteristics of the politically active and inactive.

With those objectives in mind, the study will proceed along two lines of inquiry: first, a review of related political science, gerontological and other pertinent literature; and second, a survey of 106 older Mexican-Americans in San Jose, California. Specific areas of review in the first line of inquiry are Hispanic politics, the politics of aging, political psychology and political sociology. The review of literature identifies specific issues to be examined and possible sources of variation the survey can explore, all of which lead to the development of the hypotheses to be tested. The second line of inquiry provides the actual data from which the objectives of the study can be pursued. This data will be supplemented with information from secondary sources such as the 1980 census.

Chapter I presents the nature of the problem, its relevance to gerontology and political science, and an examination of age as a variable in political behavior. Chapter II presents the concepts necessary for examining the political attitudes and participation of the study sample, possible sources of variation in participation and hypotheses to be examined through the survey. Chapter III describes the study findings, and Chapters IV and V provide an analysis of the politically active and inactive Hispanic elders and present an illustration of their personal experiences. Chapter VI concludes the study with a discourse on the potential for political activity and the implications for politics, policy and research.

The Nature of the Problem

Political participation--whether through interest in politics, voting, membership in organizations or participation in other areas--is an important characteristic of the American political system. It permits the citizenry to affect the political structures and processes (i.e.,through interest groups and political parties) and allows the political system (i.e., through politics and laws) to be responsive to the interests of the participants. Political participation in recent years has led to the growth of special interest groups organized around specific goals and affiliated with individuals of similar characteristics. Women, minorities and the elderly are examples of groups engaged in special interest politics. Through increased political activity, Hispanics in general, who face social and economic problems, are making the political system responsive to their needs (Garcia, 1973; Steiner, 1969; Holmes, 1967; Moore, 1970). In the same manner, older Hispanics, who face a variety of problems and challenges, can also make the political system and Hispanics in general responsive to their social, economic and cultural needs. For example, the elderly Hispanic not only is old, but is a member of a minority group and in many cases, is non-English speaking. This triple jeopardy can present obstacles that are difficult to overcome. These obstacles include inadequate income, little or no education and an inability to deal with a social and political system insensitive to his culture and language.

The 1980 census reveals a total of 14.6 million Hispanics in the United States with 2.6 million in the Northeast, 1.28 million in the north Central (Midwest), 4.47 million in the South and 6.25 million in the West. California has the greatest number of Hispanics (4.5 million), followed by Texas and New York (U.S. Bureau of the Census, 1981a).

A 1979 study found that 60.6 percent of Hispanics in the United States are of Mexican origin, 14.5 percent are of Puerto Rican origin, 6.6 percent are of Cuban origin, and 7.0 percent are of Central or South American origin. That same study found that the elderly Hispanics (sixty-five years and over) make up 4.5 percent of the total population of Hispanics--about 539 thousand persons. Of this group 50.6 percent (272 thousand) are of Mexican origin, 16.7 percent (90 thousand) are of Cuban origin, 8.1 percent (44 thousand) are of Puerto Rican origin, 5.2 percent (28 thousand) are of Central and South American origin, and 19.4 percent (105 thousand) are of some other Spanish origin (U.S. Bureau of Census, 1979). In comparison, the 1980 census found 11.3 percent of the general population and 6.3 percent of the non-White population to be over sixty-five (U.S. Bureau of Census, 1981a).

Like the elderly in general, the older Hispanic faces socioeconomic problems. The median income for all Americans of Spanish-speaking origin sixty-five years and older in 1978 was 3,454 dollars, compared with the median income of 5,526 dollars for the total

6

population sixty-five years and over. The incidence of poverty among the Spanish-speaking elderly is even greater than for the total Spanish-speaking populations. While 20.4 percent of Spanish-speaking persons are below the low income line, 21.9 percent of the Hispanic elderly are below that line (U.S. Bureau of Census, 1980).

The same study shows that 44.7 percent of the Hispanic elderly have completed fewer than five years of school. For Hispanics in general the figure is 17.6 percent. Among all Americans sixty-five years and older, only 9.6 percent have had fewer than five years of schooling.

In addition to income and education, Hispanic elderly face a variety of problems associated with health, transportation and housing. They have greater problems with transportation and mobility and higher incidences of poor health and substandard housing (Torres-Gil, et al., 1978; Torres-Gil, et al., 1976; Newquist, et al., 1979). They are more likely to underutilize public benefits and programs due to a lack of bilingual and bicultural services and programs and prohibitive geographic location of facilities, lack of resources with which to financially obtain needed services and lack of staff trained to work with them (Guttman, 1980; Cuellar and Weeks, 1980).

Health related problems constitute a critical obstacle in the ability of older Hispanics to face aging with independence and dignity. Surveys conducted by the National Center for Health Statistics suggest that the health of the Hispanic population aged sixty-five and over, may not be as good as that of persons of all races in the same age group, but that older Hispanics are less likely to visit doctors or dentists or to be hospitalized. The Hispanic group aged sixty-five and over had fewer dental and physician visits--when measured by proportion with one visit or more--than the comparable population of all races, even though a higher proportion of Hispanics perceived their health as fair or poor (U.S. Department of Health and Human Services, 1981).

Cultural Dilemmas

In addition to social, economic and health problems, the Hispanic elderly--unlike most elderly groups--face specific circumstances that stem from

7

their cultural and historical position as a non-English speaking minority group. Their inability to speak English (and at times their preference to speak Spanish) and their lack of understanding of "the system" is directly related to their lack of access to health, housing, recreation, employment and social services. The cultural heritage and traditional values of older Hispanics also create unique circumstances, especially since these values may come into conflict with a ₂predominantly English speaking "American" culture.² The Hispanic elderly are considered to have a subculture composed of both Mexican and American cultural elements and social-psychological elements distinctive to the experiences of elderly persons. Valle and Martinez (1981) described the conceptual characteristics of the Mexicano culture as consisting of: 1) common language and symbols in use within particular groups; 2) identifiable patterns of social relations and indigenous organization structures; and 3) shared values and beliefs.

Various studies on Hispanic elderly have found the cultural characteristics of that group to be composed of several elements including family structure, language, religion, grandparenting roles and age-related values stressing age integrated activities versus age-segregated activities. For example, the grandparenting role among Hispanics in rural Mexican-American families consists of three primary roles: religious advocates and teachers, child rearers and participants in family decision making (Leonard, 1967; Sotomayor, 1973). In addition, Hispanic elders have been found to have greater intergenerational activities within the family and to be less likely than Whites or Blacks to segregate their older members. In a large scale survey researchers found that a substantially greater proportion of older Mexican-Americans than older Blacks or Whites are living in intergenerational environments (Torres-Gil, et al., 1978). It has also been shown that Hispanics perceive the onset of old age as occurring earlier than do Anglos, partly because of the early onset of poor health (Bengtson, Cuellar and Ragan, 1977; Newton and Ruiz, 1981).

The maintenance of these cultural and linguistic characteristics, however, varies according to the Hispanic subgroup, their level of assimilation, recency of arrival to the United States, place of birth and geographic location. For example, Mexican-American

8

elderly in Los Angeles may be more likely to know English and to use it, than Puerto Rican elderly in Puerto Rico and Cuban elderly in Miami, Florida.

Among the important commonalities of this population, however, is the prevalence of an extended family. Extended families among Hispanics consist of immediate blood relations (sisters, brothers, uncles, aunts), more distant blood relations (second and third cousins) and non-blood relations such as compadres and comadres (co-parents). The traditional family structure generally reflects this form and provides the grandparenting roles listed previously (Bell, Kasschau, and Zellman, 1976). Elderly members are spared physical and psychological vulnerability (e.g., loneliness, depression), perform specific grandparenting roles, are provided economic support and assistance with housekeeping by adult children and in general, are valued members of the family.

In addition to the importance of the family to an older Hispanic, there also exist natural supportive networks that provide assistance to older Hispanics outside the family. Valle and Martinez (1981) described three types: a) aggregate networks--large or small group associations that confer rights of participation to individual members as well as defined obligation to the membership as a whole; b) link person networks--comprised of mutually linked individuals who are bound by ties of friendship based on reciprocity and exchange behaviors; and c) kinship networks--composed of individuals with family ties extending through several degrees of such a relationship, officially and unofficially adopted into the nuclear or extended family. Examples of these supportive networks include community based organizations (for example, Community Services Organization--CSO), the servidor (neighborhood helper) and the compadre.

The extent to which the traditional family structure and natural supportive networks continue to exist in rural and urban areas is uncertain and debatable. Maldonado (1975) argues that popular attitudes toward elderly Hispanics are based on concepts that have changed and are still changing. He feels that the concept of older Hispanic's deriving support from traditional support systems is untrue and misleading; that it is used as a rationale by some social workers and policymakers to justify the

9

exclusion of older Hispanics from social services.

Other Hispanics researchers, however, argue that traditional support systems are basically intact and still serve important functions (Sotomayor, 1973; Velez, 1973). Sotomayor found in a Denver study that 95 percent of older Mexican-Americans expected relatives to take care of them, either in their own home or in the relative's home, if they could no longer care for themselves. In a Los Angeles study evidence was found that older Hispanics--more so than Anglo or Black elderly--continue to have extended family orientations and hold traditional attitudes about intergenerational family roles and relationships (Torres-Gil, et al., 1978). Valle and Mendoza (1978), on the other hand, found that elderly Latinos in San Diego are less traditional in their attitudes toward the role of the family; however, they did rely on support from family members in times of need.

In spite of conflicting claims about the continued reliance on traditional family structures among older Hispanics, it is becoming apparent that assimilation and upward mobility by younger Hispanics, increased costs of housing, high inflation, and greater dispersion of Hispanic neighborhoods are having a deleterious effect on the elderly. Solis's research (1975) supports the contention that extended family structures and social support systems among Hispanics are eroding, so that today a significant number of elderly Hispanics are isolated both residentially and socially and are vulnerable to institutionalization. In large urban areas such as Los Angeles, New York, Chicago and Miami it is apparent that older Hispanics increasingly are living alone and are forced to rely upon their own resources for support.

Social Policies for the Elderly

With the demise of the extended family in some locations, the increasing alienation of older Hispanics from their families and the growing isolation from their culture and community, what social supports are available to older Hispanics? In the last ten years, as social policies and programs have developed for the elderly, federal and state governments have begun to recognize the diversity among the elderly population, the unique circumstances of Hispanic older persons and the vulnerability they face in an increasingly complex and technological world. This recognition did not

10

always exist. Over the years a host of programs for the elderly has been created, ranging from Social Security and Medicare to housing and transporation programs, physical and mental health services and a variety of supportive social services under the Older Americans Act of 1965 and Title XX of the Social Security Act. These programs, however, were predicated on the assumption that a homogeneous population of older persons existed and that any services provided to an essentially English speaking population would eventually reach all minority groups, including Blacks, Asians, Indians and Hispanics (Torres-Gil & Negm, 1980). In some cases a myth existed that "minorities take care of their own." Maldonado (1975), in describing the situation of older Hispanics, noted that such a stereotype existed about Hispanics, thus providing a rationale for social service providers to ignore their needs. In the same way, service providers and professionals, reflecting unofficial assumptions, may not have attached a priority to the needs of older Hispanics because of a continuing belief that the extended family existed with its concomitant emotional, social and financial supports. [3] Various events such as the 1971 White House Conference on Aging and pressures from minority and Hispanic professionals--as well as the enlightened response of government officials--led to efforts to provide preferences and targeted services to minority elderly who faced linguistic, cultural and social needs (Owens, et al., 1973).

As a result of those events, major gains for the minority elderly began to occur during the 1970s. The 1973 amendments to the Older Americans Act acknowledged that older persons are heterogeneous. Federal regulations specifically singled out the "low income elderly and minority elderly" as recipients of social services. Area agencies on aging and other social programs began to create nutrition projects, multipurpose centers and transportation and housing programs, which were located in areas with large concentrations of Hispanics or were composed of Spanish speaking professionals and staff. That did not always occur in proportion with the needs of Spanish speaking elderly for those services, and it varied according to states, with California providing a high level of services. In 1978 the amendments were revised to provide preference to "those with the greatest economic or social needs." The regulations provided for "cultural and linguistic needs" of

11

minority seniors, thus continuing to recognize that heterogeneity existed.[4] Those legislative and regulatory initiatives contributed to the development of research on Hispanic aging, to the growth of Hispanic organizations supporting the Spanish speaking elderly and to the increasing sensitivity of public and elected officials to the growing numbers of Hispanic elderly and their diverse needs. These trends indicated that major gains would continue and that federal services would begin to supplant the loss of traditional support services.

By 1980 it was clear that trend was in jeopardy. Until this time sensitivity to the needs of Hispanic elderly was predominantly that of professionals and federal officials. With the election of a Republican administration and the resulting "New Federalism" with its philosophy of greater local and state control, decentralization of federal oversight and creation of block grants, many of the gains of the 1970s were beginning to disappear. Funding cutbacks in federal programs drastically curtailed transportation, legal assistance, housing, nutrition and other supportive services for the elderly. Deregulation of many federal agencies resulted in less federal monitoring and less attention to specific subgroups of the population, which in turn created a situation whereby older Hispanics no longer could depend on the sensitivity and advocacy of professionals and public officials (many of whom had lost their jobs) to ensure that cultural and linguistically related services would be provided. Those events and trends led to the situation older Hispanics now face: the worst of all worlds.

Multiple Jeopardy: The Worst of All Worlds

As urbanization and assimilation take their toll on the traditional support systems for the elderly Hispanic and as government reduces supportive services, he may become more isolated and may be forced to rely even more on his own limited resources to obtain the assistance necessary to all elderly persons. Such assistance includes the means for securing adequate maintenance including food, shelter and clothing; maintenance of physical and mental health, with support and care from other persons in the event of ill health; opportunities for continued useful and meaningful activity; and a reasonable measure of individual choice in the ways his needs are to be satisfied--choices of where to live and work and how to use leisure time.

Unless those needs are met, the dilemma between the older Hispanic's traditional reliance on the extended family, supportive natural networks, barrio (neighborhood) and church and his growing reliance on governmental support systems (which do not always address themselves to the needs of this subgroup and are now being cut back) will create problems and will necessitate some form of action to solve the problems. Velez refers to those issues when he describes a contradiction that "exists between his (the aged Hispanic's) inner social and cultural world and the outer world's cultural and social structure" (Velez, 1973:13). The inner world, according to Velez, is the traditional world within the home and barrio where the older Hispanic has had meaningful roles, status and authority and has received necessary social and physical support. The outer world is a White oriented, English-speaking system that is insensitive to the older Hispanic's physical and cultural needs:

> ... like the rest of the elderly population, there will be an increase of larger and larger groups of Chicano elderly and from my point of view the essential contradictions described cannot continue nor can they be permitted to be sustained. If they are allowed to be sustained, I would suggest that elderly Chicanos may well begin to fill the halls of mental institutions, or increased conflicts with Mexican families will occur resulting in greater and greater cleavages between family members, and ultimately a serious departure from a social and cultural system which provided sustenance to a group of people who have long faced institutional prejudice and economic exploitation. (Velez, 1973:13).

In another article, Velez (1981) discusses the direct relation those trends and dislocations have on mental health. Velez refers to the negative effects of structural changes upon cultural systems as the "delocalization" of such systems, as opposed to images created by "modernization" or "urbanization" theories, which tend to perceive such changes as inevitable and evolutionary. Delocalization is the process by which an adaptive cultural system is uprooted from its context--urban or rural--by structural changes and with it the social processes which persons have engaged and maintained in growing old.

13

It is his belief that the societal changes affecting traditional culture and support mechanisms lead to a situation whereby accumulated relationships, statuses and roles and social interdependences characterizing a cultural system are either destroyed or significantly altered. In turn, this change creates a situation whereby the older person suffers poor mental health and a loss in esteem, self concept, and personal control and isolation and loneliness.

Therefore, a dilemma exists. With the combination of losses in traditional supports; assimilation among the Hispanic population, which modifies cultural characteristics; a change in governmental philosophies, which place older Hispanics in a position of multiple jeopardy; less reliance on the family; and fewer social supports; the Hispanic older person is faced with some difficult choices: to accept that situation, to cope individually or to adapt to changing circumstances and attempt to affect his or her environment.

Benefits from Involvement

Velez suggests an alternative to this scenario, an alternative used by White elderly: that the Hispanic elderly mobilize in political activity with other elderly persons to implement public goals that have as their central foci strategies to eliminate the difficulties described above.[5] Political activity by older Hispanics could have two purposes: first, to influence public policy to provide social services designed for a Spanish speaking, Hispanic heritage population; second, to provide an integral role for los Ancianos within general Hispanic politics.

Whether the older Hispanic is involved in politics is unclear from the literature of political science and gerontology. In a review of the available literature on the Hispanic aged prior to 1972, Torres-Gil (1972) found fewer than thirty published and unpublished articles. Most of the writings dealt with housing and communication or transportation as related issues. Since then, an increase in interest and research, and hence in publications, has occurred in Hispanic gerontology, but only a few have dealt with Hispanic elderly and political participation.

Among the numerous articles in ethnicity and aging, there are only a few that have dealt with politics and Hispanic elderly. Torres-Gil and Becerra

14

(1977) have discussed the political attitudes and participation of older Mexican-Americans. They found that overall political activity is low among Mexican-American elderly due to a sense of low political efficacy. They also found two major areas of concern affecting this sense of low efficacy: environmental barriers (low income, low educational attainment, poor health, lack of citizenship) and perceived barriers (discrimination has served to generate a perception that political activity is either useless or associated with personal risk). Velez et al., (1981) describes the interaction between political participation of Hispanic elderly and mental health as expressed by life satisfaction.

Although several books exist on Chicano politics and numerous articles now deal with this subject, again, few have focused on the role of the Hispanic older person in the growing political activism of Hispanics or on their role in the political process.

The politics of aging, a growing area, has much to say about the attitudes, participation and role of the elderly in political activities, however, there has been little mention of Hispanic elderly. Holtzman (1963), Pinner, Jacobs, and Selznick (1959) and Putnam (1970) describe the rise of the Townsend Movement and the McClain Organization in California during the Depression and post World War II as they sought to gain political influence for older persons. Pratt (1976) examines the politics of contemporary aging based organizations, specifically the National Council of Senior Citizens, National Retired Teachers Association/American Association of Retired Persons (NRTA/AARP) and the National Association of Retired Federal Employees (NARFE) and their efforts to influence aging policies and programs. In a review of the literature dealing with the origins, internal characteristics and political activities of aged based organizations, Hudson and Binstock conclude that "there are a great many aging based organizations about which little is known other than through statements written by the organizations" (1976:386).[6] He specifically alludes to the creation of several minority aged based organizations: the National Caucus on Black Aged and the Asociacion Nacional Pro Personas Mayores. He recommends that further research be conducted on distinctive subgroups of the population, which seek to advocate for ethnic and minority concerns.

Various writers, however, have mentioned the need for a more active political role by the older Hispanic. For example, Gibson says in a report on the Hispanic elderly in San Antonio:

> Where his interest is of concern he plays little or no part in community politics .... If he is to form a power faction he must organize to demand active participation and control of local, state, and federal resources (Gibson, 1973:88).

Torres-Gil (1982) discusses the political potential of the older Hispanic and recommends that Hispanic political activists integrate the elderly in their efforts to acquire political power.

The limited literature available leads one to suspect that the Hispanic elderly are not active in politics. This does not mean that some of the elderly do not actively participate. In some instances older people have been leaders in the Hispanic political movements or involved in senior citizens activities. Henry Santiestevan, formerly of the Southwest Council of la Raza (now the National Council of la Raza), prophetically illustrates the potential for involvement of some elderly Mexican-Americans in Hispanic politics:

> That they are capable of change and are even found, in some cases, in the forefront of the movement is obvious. For example: they were found in the front ranks of the pilgrimage of the farmworkers from Delano to Sacramento, California; in the march from Rio Grande City to Austin, Texas, and in the march of San Felipe del Rio. From the Rio Grande Valley of Texas to the foothills of New Mexico and the urban center of East Los Angeles, you will find elderly Mexican-Americans not only participating along with the youth in the movement for social change, but adding to it their years of wisdom and experience. (U.S. Congress, 1970:590)

Nonetheless, fragmentary evidence suggests that the Hispanic aged in general may be relatively inactive in various forms of politics, including political interest, voting, participation beyond voting and political leadership.

16

In contrast, the White elderly and Hispanics in general are relatively active in politics.[7] Table 1 shows that persons sixty-five years old and over in 1960, 1964 and 1968 were at least as active as those twenty-one to twenty-nine years of age in voting, contributing money to a political party, attending political meetings and working for a party. Woodward and Roper (1950) found also that people fifty years old and over rated at least as high as younger persons on an index of political activity (voting, discussing public issues, writing to congressmen) in 1950 (see Table 2). One of the most active forms of political activity is participation in groups. According to Hausknecht (1962), the proportion of voluntary association members who belong to political and pressure associations constitute some 5 percent of persons aged fifty-five and over, in comparison with 4 percent of those aged twenty-one to thirty-four and 3 percent of those aged thirty-five to fifty-four (see Table 3).

In addition, older people give more attention than young people to electoral campaigns covered in the mass media and are more likely than the young to follow public affairs and news through newspaper reading and television viewing (Riley & Foner, 1968).

Data from the 1980 election show that voting and registration rates were high among the White elderly. It was found that 78 percent of those between fifty-five and seventy-four were registered to vote in that election; furthermore, 71 percent of the elderly did vote. In contrast, that same study showed that only 50 percent of the Hispanic elderly were registered to vote, and that only 43 percent actually voted (U.S. Bureau of Census, 1981b).

Data about political participation of Hispanics are not as extensive as data about the white elderly. Cross sectional studies on voting and other political activities engaged in by Hispanics generally cover limited geographical areas: Texas, Los Angeles and parts of Nebraska. Table 4 shows that registration rates in fifteen Texas counties with Mexican-American majorities during the 1960s were at about the same levels as, or were sometimes higher than, the rates for the state as a whole. On the other hand, the turnout of registered voters in the Hispanic counties was usually 3 to 15 percent below that of the entire state. In addition to registration and voting,

17

TABLE 1

PARTICIPATION IN POLITICS BY AGE GROUPS
(Percentage)

Age	Voted in Presidential Elections	Gave Money to Party	Attended Political Meeting	Worked for Party	Wore Campaign Button	Supported Party in Conversation
21-29	58	7	7	4	16	32
30-39	72	10	10	7	21	32
40-49	77	10	9	6	17	30
50-64	73	10	6	4	13	27
65 & over	68	8	7	4	7	24

SOURCE: Campbell (1971:113). Data from the Survey Research Center's Surveys of the National Electorate in 1960, 1964, and 1968.

TABLE 2

AMOUNT OF POLITICAL ACTIVITY EXHIBITED
BY VARIOUS AGE GROUPS
(Percentage)

Age	Very Active	Fairly Active	Fairly Inactive	Very Inactive
21-34	8	14	32	46
35-49	11	19	39	31
50&over	12	17	34	37
Total adult population	10	17	35	38

SOURCE: Woodward and Roper (1950:877).

TABLE 3

DISTRIBUTION OF VOLUNTARY ASSOCIATION MEMBERS
BY TYPE OF ASSOCIATION AND AGE[a]
(Percentage)

Type of Association	Age 21-34	Age 35-54	Age 55 & Over
Veterans	15	13	16
Civic	49	42	20
Political	4	3	5
Lodges	20	32	40
Church	20	25	31
Economic	9	7	9
Cultural	4	4	3
Social	21	14	14
Total N	234	384	221

SOURCE: Hausknecht (1962:85)

[a]Voluntary associations are defined as including the
following groups: veterans, military, and patriotic
organizations related to health, civic or service,
political or pressure groups, lodges, fraternal,
church, religious, economic, occupational, professional, cultural, educational, social, recreational.

TABLE 4

VOTER REGISTRATION AND TURNOUT IN TEXAS IN
PREDOMINANTLY MEXICAN-AMERICAN COUNTIES,
1960-1970
(Percentage)

Year	Registration as Percentage of Adult Population, 1960		Voter Turnout as Percentage of Registered Voters	
	State	Mexican-American Counties	State	Mexican-American Counties
1960	46.9	46.5	89.1	79.0
1962	42.9	44.3	63.6	65.4
1964	50.5	51.4	87.1	76.0
1966	48.3	53.2	48.1	40.6
1968	64.0	65.1	75.6	60.7
1970	63.2	69.6	53.9	47.9

SOURCE: McCleskey and Merrill (1973:787)

21

participation rates by Texas Mexican-Americans in 1969, on an index of other political activities (see Table 5), were lower than those for Blacks and Whites.

In the Mexican-American study project conducted in the 1960s by the University of California at Los Angeles, voting and registration rates for Mexican-Americans in San Antonio and Los Angeles were even lower than those found in the Texas survey. San Antonio had 46.3 percent registered and 38.1 percent who actually had voted, while Los Angeles County had 55.9 percent registered and 49.9 percent who actually had voted (Grebler et al., 1970: 564).[8]

Another study of Chicano political participation in four Nebraska Chicano population centers (Welch et al., 1973) found that on some political activities (such as putting bumper stickers on cars or belonging to political clubs or organizations), Hispanic participation was comparable to or higher than the national average (see Table 6). General political interest was also found to be relatively high. These findings are surprising, because political participation is generally assumed to be related to education and social status, and the Nebraska sample had a lower educational and income level than the national average. In other activities (such as talking to people about a candidate or an issue, or attendance at political rallies) participation of those sampled was much lower than the national average.

Voting and registration rates for Hispanics are lower than for the general population. In a national study of these rates in the November, 1980 election, it was found that 36.3 percent of Hispanics were registered to vote and 29.9 percent of Hispanics voted. Overall, 82.2 percent of the Hispanics who were registered did vote. This compares to 88.6 percent for the general population. Of the adult Hispanics, 32.2 percent did not vote in that election because they were not U.S. citizens (U.S. Bureau of the Census, 1981b).

Information and publications on Hispanic politics show that Hispanics still face obstacles toward effective voter registration, voting and influence in the political system. In the last decade, however, they have steadily increased their participation and effectiveness. In 1982, there were approximately eight Hispanic Congressmen. Organizations advocating and lobbying for Hispanics on a political basis have

22

TABLE 5

POLITICAL PARTICIPATION IN TEXAS, NOVEMBER 1969

(Percentage)

Participation	Anglo (N=797)	Negro (N=419)	Mexican-American (N=375)
Held party office	2	1	2
Given money to campaign	24	16	11
Attended political rallies	32	18	22
Worked for candidates	24	21	13
How often do you talk politics with friends?			
Frequently	27	23	14
Sometimes	27	31	32
Seldom	35	28	32
Never	9	16	22

SOURCE: McCleskey and Merrill (1973:789).

TABLE 6

LEVELS OF POLITICAL PARTICIPATION: SOME COMPARISONS
(Percentage)

Participation	Mexican-Americans	Southern Whites	Southern Blacks	National Sample
Talk about politics with:				
Family (N=177)	69	64	76	--
Friends (N=177)	56	76	84	--
Neighbors (N=161)	21	--	--	--
Priest or minister (N=156)	27	--	--	--
Community leaders (N=175)	19	41	28	--
Government bureaucrats (N=175)	8	--	--	--
Public officials (N=175)	14	--	--	--
During campaigns (N=174)				
Talk to people about candidate or issues	10	--	--	33
Work for candidate or party	7	--	--	5
Put bumper sticker on car	17	--	--	15
Collect money for a candidate	3	--	--	12
Attend a political rally	3	--	--	14
Belong to a club or organization	9	3	10	3

SOURCE: Welch et al. (1973:803).

24

proliferated, and state and local areas with high Hispanic concentrations increasingly have become organized. The present strength of the Hispanic community is estimated at three million registered voters in 1980, concentrated in key states with large numbers of electoral votes. Although articles allude to the low Hispanic turnout at the polls and voter registration drives, the surfacing of attractive Hispanic candidates and an increasing Hispanic middle class have begun to raise voter registration and voting rates (Pachon, 1982).

Although the data on Hispanic political participation cover limited geographic areas and are not comprehensive they do indicate that Hispanics in general are active in various political activities. In comparison with the suspected political inactivity of the Hispanic elderly and their lower levels of registration and voting, the White elderly and Hispanics in general are politically active.

This study will attempt to determine the actual extent of political participation among a sample of Hispanic elderly and to compare these rates with those of the White elderly and Hispanics in general. The study also will examine sources of variation among the Hispanic elderly. For example, why are some Hispanic elders politically active and others politically inactive? What factors impede political participation among older Hispanics?

Before examining specific factors that may account for inactivity among older Hispanics, one must note that age in itself is not a barrier to participation among older persons. If it was, the potential for older persons becoming politically active would be limited. Among younger Hispanic activists, one often hears such comments as "that (older) person is too old; why should we work with him?" or "older people do not care about politics because at their age it doesn't matter anymore." These comments, of course, are based on stereotypes and ignorance; they negate the possibility of evoking the interest of older Hispanics in issues important to them as citizens, as Hispanics and as elderly persons. Therefore, before considering factors that hinder participation among older Hispanics, one must show that age as a variable does not predict apathy or low political participation.

The Effect of Age on Political Behavior

In a comprehensive review of literature on the political attitudes and behaviors of the older person, Hudson and Binstock examined the effects of age on political participation among the elderly:

> Many forms of political participation do not decline in old age. And, even though some cross-sectional data indicate that older persons are less active politically than younger ones, a number of studies show lower levels of political activity to be more a function of female sex and low education than of age. The aged are less involved in the more active forms of participation, but it seems quite certain this results more from physical infirmity and lack of mobility rather than from any significant falling off in interest about political matters (Hudson and Binstock, 1976:374).

Hudson and Binstock substantiate their position by describing a variety of studies that show that age does not impede political participation. For example, studies show a roughly linear relationship between age and political interest; political interest tends to increase with advancing age (Lazarsfeld et al., 1944; Berelson et al., 1954). Glenn and Grimes (1968) and Glenn (1969), in controlling for sex and education, found a positive monotonic relationship between age and reported political interest. Glenn (1969), when controlling for education, also found no appreciable variation by age in interest or opinion making. He concluded that as they get older, people become neither less interested in national and international affairs nor less likely to express their opinions to interviewers.

Studies of the voting behavior of older persons consistently show that voting participation increased with age and peaked in their early sixties but never fell back to the lower levels of the twenties and early thirties (Milbrath, 1965; Crittenden, 1963; Glenn and Grimes, 1968; Verba and Nie, 1972). Where control such as education, sex and income were introduced, fall-off after age sixty diminished, and in some cases voting rates increased after age sixty (Glenn & Grimes, 1971; U.S. Bureau of the Census, 1971; Verba & Nie, 1972; Nie et al., 1974). For example, when they introduced

26

controls for both sex and education, Glenn and Grimes (1968) found that the moderate decrease reported after the fifties was either reversed or eliminated for persons from aged fifty to eighty. When controlling for socioeconomic status and length of residency, Verba and Nie (1972) found no decline in interest for even the oldest group.

In forms of participation more active than voting (e.g., attending meetings, contacting officials, being an active member of a party, soliciting funds), the participation rates of older persons compared to those of younger persons were similar to those found in voting. When controls for education, sex, residency and overall socioeconomic status were introduced, age as a variable in explaining lower participation among older persons became less important. In a national population survey, Verba and Nie (1972) found in overall participation a pattern of increase from their twenties to the forties, followed by a decline, although at age sixty-five, persons still participated more than those in their twenties.[9]

In voting, the same general pattern held true, although the decline started around age fifty rather than age forty. However, Verba and Nie (1972) postulated that socioeconomic factors (education, income, occupation), and not age alone, were responsible for the decline in both overall participation past the age of forty and voting past the age of fifty. With the correction for socioeconomic status, overall participation declined much less by age. For voting, participation corrected for socioeconomic status actually increased for older persons rather than declined. Nie et al.'s (1974) cross national study reveals that participation during the life cycle rose through the early years, peaked during middle age and fell later in life. With education controlled, the activity scores for the oldest group were higher in each of the countries except Japan, and the downturn in participation was either substantially reduced (United States and Nigeria) or eliminated altogether (India). They also controlled for retirement and found that those who were still active in the work force participated more than those who were not (India, Japan, and the United States).

In general, these studies show that age itself does not hinder political participation. When age is

27

isolated as a variable by controlling for sex and education, interest in politics increases with age and never diminishes. Voting participation increases until age sixty and then falls off somewhat. In more active forms of political participation, older persons are involved nearly as much as all adults except in such activities as working to form groups to deal with general local problems and taking active roles in such organizations.

The literature also raises questions about the political orientation of older persons, with speculations being raised that they may become more conservative with age (Glenn, 1974). Age differences in political beliefs and attitudes are shown by survey data to be generally smaller than popularly supposed. There is little evidence of systematic movement toward conservatism as people move through the life cycle (Campbell, 1971; Butler and Stokes, 1971). The proposition that American elderly are politically more conservative than the middle-aged was tested, and in general, the differences between the two groups appear small (Campbell and Strate, 1981). People of all ages respond to political issues and events in terms of their early socialization and their immediate social and economic circumstances.

Politics of Aging

Political participation has translated into the development of senior citizen political movements and aged based organizations. As described earlier, a variety of movements and organizations have been developed to advocate for older persons. In turn, they are having a dramatic impact on the formulation and implementation of public policy. Hudson (1981) presents case studies of their impact on programs such as Medicare, Social Security, Supplemental Security Income, the Older Americans Act, and long term care; and he documents the influence older persons and their advocacy organizations have had on those programs. The White House Conferences on Aging in 1961, 1971 and 1981 reflect the development of older persons as an important political constituency. The conferences have served to galvanize and organize seniors to pressure the Congress and Executive Branch to provide greater benefits for older persons. To some extent, the White House Conferences on Aging have directly or indirectly influenced the passages of Medicare, the Older Americans Act and Supplemental Security Income

28

and also the creation of the Administration on Aging and the National Institute on Aging, as well as the development of nutrition programs. Organized activities on behalf of older persons have led to increased benefits and a greater share of federal resources. In 1981 it was estimated that 28 percent of the federal budget directly or indirectly resulted in benefits for older persons (including Social Security benefits) (Samuelson, 1981).

Although studies on the political participation of older persons and reports about their organized efforts have not utilized samples or focused on Spanish-speaking elderly, one may assume that age will not be a barrier to participation among those groups and that they have potential for promoting the politics of Hispanic aging. In other words, Spanish speaking elderly, to the extent that conditions necessary for participation are present, do have the potential to be active participants and engage in organized activities. However, since data are not available on the politics of elderly Hispanics, it is difficult at this point to state whether they are, in fact, as politically active as older persons in general and what cultural, attitudinal or socioeconomic factors might account for variation in participation among them. In the next chapter, theories of political culture and political socialization will be used to consider the political orientations and political behavior older Hispanics can be expected to exhibit given their cultural background, historical developments and socioeconomic situation. Based on this examination, hypotheses will be developed that specify factors affecting current rates of political participation found among older Hispanics.

1. Throughout the book the terms "Hispanic" (and "Spanish-speaking") will be used to reflect all persons of Spanish-speaking origin in the United States (Puerto Ricans, Cubans, Latin Americans and Mexican-Americans). In recent years several descriptive terms have been used to refer to specific subgroups of Hispanics: Mexican-American or Chicano, Puerto Rican, Cuban, Latino, Central American. The term "Hispanic" is a widely accepted description for those groups. When referring specifically to Hispanics in San Jose and other parts of California, however, the term "Mexican-American" will be used. It should be noted that Mexican-American elderly do not generally refer to themselves as Chicanos, but rather as Mexicanos, Mexican-Americans or Hispanos (Hispanics). Older Mexican-Americans have a different meaning for the word "Chicano": a person of low status, while younger Chicanos use the word to signify a politically and culturally aware person.

2. Newton and Ruiz provide a broad perspective on the construct "culture" by referring to "a system of shared artifacts, psychological experiences, and social variables" (1981:49-50). They further define cultural groups by linguistic, racial, historical and national bonds, which may be comprised of subgroups, each possessing a distinctive subset of the cultural system of the total group.

3. In a study of the social participation of Black elderly, Daniel Rubenstein (1971) states that "while this need is known, it has not been fully accepted" (p. 2). He cites several studies that show that the heterogeneity of the elderly population is not sufficiently recognized. For example, in "Social Relations of Widows in Black and White Urban Communities" (AoA publication No.25, U.S. Department of Health, Education and Welfare, SRS, AoA, limited circulation, undated) Helena A. Lopata found that difference generally was addressed through a model drawn from middle-class whites, usually of Protestant background and assimilated "blend," reinforced by life cycle generalizations and the disengagement theory. Robert G. Havighurst ("A Report of a Special Committee of the Gerontological Society," The Gerontologist, 9, no.4, part 2 (Winter, 1971:85) noted that one of the major shortcomings of many present programs for the

aged is that they aim too much at involving a broad base of persons without considering the needs of various population subgroups.

4. Intense debate has developed over the definition of "greatest economic or social needs." Minority organizations preferred the earlier definition, giving preference to minority and poor elderly, while other organizations felt that a broader definition was needed to incorporate all older persons, regardless of race or income. A final decision was made in 1980, defining "greatest social need" as the need caused by non-economic factors--which include physical and mental disabilities, language barriers, cultural or social isolation including that caused by racial or ethnic status--which restrict an individual's ability to perform normal daily tasks or which threaten his or her capacity to live independently. "Greatest economic need" was defined as the need resulting from an income level at or below the poverty threshold established by the Bureau of the Census.

5. Political activity by White elderly is characterized by the relatively high degree of political participation among individuals and the large number of age-related organizations (see Chapter VI).

6. An aging based organization is defined by Hudson and Binstock as one that depends in large measure for its activities upon the existence of older persons as membership for the organizations; as consumers of the organization's goods and services or those offered by its members; as clients for the practitioners who belong to the organization; or as subjects for study by researchers and educators who comprise the organizations membership (1976:381).

7. Many White older persons are second and third generation immigrants in the United States whereas, most Hispanic elderly, with the exception of those descended from old Spanish and Mexican families, would probably be recent "immigrants" or first generation in this country. Therefore, it would be expected that since White elderly have had more exposure to political stimuli in this country and are more accustomed to the political system, they would be more active politically than the Hispanic elderly. However, since data on rates of political activity among first and second generation Germans, Italians and other White ethnic groups currently residing in this country are largely

unavailable, the study will compare rates between older Hispanics and elderly White persons.

8. The higher rate of political participation in Los Angeles than in San Antonio was attributed in part to the better socioeconomic position of the Los Angeles Chicano and the greater openness of the political system in Los Angeles.

9. Overall participation included communal activities -- any activity where a citizen cooperates with others, either in informal groups or formal organizations and in campaign activities -- working for a party, attending meetings, contributing money, persuading others how they should vote.

CHAPTER II

CONCEPTUAL ISSUES IN A STUDY OF
POLITICAL BEHAVIOR

Introduction

In the American political culture, persons grow up
with a sense of civic obligation and political
responsiblity. From early childhood they are
encouraged to take civics courses and to vote for
representatives in clubs, in their school classes, and
in school-wide elections. As adults they are expected
to understand local and national issues, to vote, and
to be members of civic groups. Yet participation
requires a conscious commitment and expenditure of
energy, both physical and mental, and not all persons
are politically active. A person may be incapable,
uninterested, fearful, or apathetic about politics.
External factors (social, cultural, economic, and
political) may also impede his participation.

Politically inactive individuals or groups have
been the subjects of countless studies which have
sought to determine the causes that account for
political behavior. A variety of literature deals with
the "why" of political participation. For example,
political psychology deals with psychosocial aspects of
individual political behavior. Ethnic politics
concerns the dynamics of immigration, assimilation, and
culture on the political behavior of ethnic groups. In
general, the macro level of political science refers to
the interaction of large social units such as nations,
political systems, and organizations with each other
and with individuals. The micro level, often referred
to as the behavioral study of politics, refers to
individuals and their political behavior. The micro
and macro literature dealing directly and indirectly
with individual political behavior agrees that a person
must in some way be motivated to participate in
political action.[1]

If motivation does not exist, then an individual
will neither make the necessary commitment nor expend
the energy required. Motivation implies several
important considerations. First, a person must feel he
has a stake in the political system. He must have a
sense of involvement, a personal interest; thus, the

33

rituals, forms, rules, and content must appeal to him. He must feel that he belongs in the society. This feeling of involvement is also concerned with specific issues; he must care about the outcome. Second, a person must have a sense of political efficacy; he must feel his action will make a difference. Without a sense of efficacy a person will feel his actions are not worthwhile; hence he will be less likely to participate. If he is sick, lacks transportation, cannot read or write the language, or is not a citizen, he will be incapable of participating. A sense of involvement in the political system, a sense of efficacy, and access are important if an individual is to be motivated to participate. If any one or all three of these factors are missing, an individual will probably remain politically inactive. For some older Hispanics the estrangement is particularly severe. Many have been deliberately excluded and forcibly prevented from participation: repression and political gerrymandering in the Southwest, forced deportations, and zoot suit riots in Los Angeles during World War II, have created a climate of fear among some Hispanics who are now older, which in turn, makes it more difficult for them to feel they can effectively and safely participate in political activities.

For the elderly Hispanic these factors take on special significance. If the older Hispanic feels he does not belong in this country or has no right to be here, he will not feel he has a right or duty to participate in the political system. If he feels he is not a part of Hispanic political activities, he will not be motivated to participate in Hispanic politics. In addition, if he feels that participation will bring him no personal benefits or if he is physically incapable of participating, he will be less likely to be active. In examining the political participation and political attitudes of the Hispanic elderly and in developing hypotheses about their suspected inactivity, one must account for all these concerns. For example, is the older Hispanic oriented toward the norms and values of the American political system? Does he feel a sense of involvement with Hispanic political activities? Is he efficacious and does he have access to participation in politics? If these questions can be answered in the affirmative, then one might expect that the older Hispanic will be relatively active. However, older Hispanics seem relatively inactive since the limited literature (Newton & Ruiz, 1981) and the writer's personal experiences point in that direction.

To understand why they might be inactive, one must
examine the political attitudes and political
participation of the older Hispanic in the context of
the theory of political culture.

The Theory of Political Culture

In an analysis of political behavior, the concept
of political culture helps to present a balanced
picture of the relative importance of socialization,
historical developments, personal experiences, and
reactions to events which affect political attitudes
and political participation. It also provides a useful
basis for examining the links between social, cultural,
and economic factors and political performance. Since
this study concerns the political behavior of older
Hispanics, an exploration of their political culture
will provide the contextual background necessary for
examining factors that have influenced their
orientation toward politics and their political
attitudes. For example, when one discusses contemporary
factors which impede political participation of elderly
Hispanics, the theory of political culture will help
describe and define the political environment in which
the older person has been raised and the socializing
agents which inducted him into his particular culture.

A political culture

is the product of both the collective history
of a political system and the life histories
of the individuals who currently make up the
system; and thus is rooted equally in public
events and private experiences. (Pye &
Verba, 1965:8)

It consists of "the system of empirical beliefs,
expressive symbols, and values which define the
situation in which political action takes place" (Pye &
Verba, 1965:513) and refers to "the specifically
political orientations-attitudes toward the political
system, and its various parts, and attitudes toward the
role of the self in the system" (Almond & Verba,
1963:12). The theory of political culture was
developed in response to the need to bridge a growing
gap in the behavioral approach in political science
between the level of micro analysis based on
psychological interpretations of the individual's
political behavior and the level of macro analysis
based on the interaction of groups, organizations, and

governmental activities (Pye & Verba, 1965:8).[2]

In their classic study of the "civic culture," Almond and Verba formulated and examined characteristics which make up the political cultures in five countries: Mexico, United States, Great Britain, Germany, and Italy. They define the political culture of a nation as the particular distribution of patterns of orientation toward political objects among the members of a nation. They state: "When we speak of the political culture of a society, we refer to the political system as internalized in the cognitions, feelings, and evaluations of its population" (Almond & Verba, 1963:13).[3] There are three "pure" (homogeneous) types of political cultures: parochial, subject, and participant. These three political cultures differ in the

> frequency of different kinds of cognitive, affective, and evaluative orientation toward the political system in general, its input and output aspects, and the self as political actor. (Almond & Verba, 1963: 14)

Homogeneous political cultures

Parochial political cultures are characterized by societies with no specific political institutions separate from religious and social institutions. The political cultures of African tribal societies fall into this category. A member of a parochial political culture expects nothing from the political system. Although he may be vaguely aware that a central political system exists, his feelings toward it are uncertain and do not encourage an active relation to it.

Subject political cultures show strong orientation toward the output aspects of the system, but orientations toward the input aspects are weak. In this system the output aspects, which predominate, are the administrative processes, usually bureaucracies and the courts, which apply or enforce authoritative policies. The input aspects, which are minimal, are the political processes by which the demands of the society flow into the polity and are converted into authoritative policies. A citizen in a subject culture does not often see himself as an active participant. He is aware of a centralized governmental authority and may like or dislike it, but his relationship with it is

36

a passive one. He neither expects nor demands that he be involved in the political parties, interest groups, or media of communication which make up the input process. In this political culture any civic obligation to be an active participant and political actor in the structure of the society is minimal.

The members of a participant political culture tend to be strongly oriented to the system as a whole, to the political and administrative structures, and to processes of the political system. The members of the participant polity are oriented toward an activist role in the polity. Participation in both the political and administrative structure becomes the norm, although the members' feelings toward specific political issues and political objects may vary from acceptance to rejection, from favorable to unfavorable. In general, the citizen of this polity is expected to be active in politics.[4]

Almond and Verba stress that their typologies of political cultures are "pure"--that is, unmixed polities which do not include a mix of political cultures. In reality, few political cultures are homogeneous and uniform. Recognizing this, Almond and Verba further subdivide their classification of political cultures into three types of mixed political cultures: (1) the parochial-subject culture, (2) the subject-participant culture, and (3) the parochial-participant culture.

Mixed political cultures

In the parochial-subject culture a substantial portion of the population is oriented toward a more centralized governmental structure and has rejected the parochial nature-tribal, village, feudal authority--of the social environment. This is exemplified by societies such as African Kingdoms and the Ottoman Empire in which parochial authority exists within a developing central governmental structure. In the mixed subject-participant culture a substantial number of citizens act as activists toward the input aspects (political processes) of the society. Simultaneously most of the remainder of the population are subject, continue to be oriented toward an authoritarian governmental structure, and have a passive set of orientations.[5] The parochial-participant culture is characteristic of many of the emerging nations of Asia and Africa. In these countries the political

culture has been predominantly parochial; but through
colonization, a participant culture has been forcibly
injected. After Britain and Belgium allowed independence, African nations clearly showed the problems
experienced by these polities. While the vast majority
of the population had been socialized as parochials,
the political structures and processes introduced by
the colonizers had been participant ones. Since few
"participants" remained to man an infrastructure or a
bureaucracy when the colonizers departed, instability
and chaos usually occurred.

The Political Cultures of the
United States and Mexico

Data from Almond and Verba's large-scale survey of
political attitudes and political participation in five
countries reveal characteristics of political cultures
of the United States and Mexico useful for
understanding the political behavior of older Hispanics
in this country.[6] Their findings indicate why
older Hispanics who have been socialized into the
Mexican political structure would not be expected to
participate actively in the American political system.

The political culture of the United States is
characterized as a civic culture. Here, the role of
the participant is highly developed and widespread.
The study found that, compared to respondents from the
other four countries (Great Britain, Germany, Italy,
Mexico), United States respondents were frequently
exposed to politics. Political discussion and
involvement were high, and a strong sense of obligation
to take an active part in the community and a sense of
competence to influence the government existed. United
States respondents were also active members of
voluntary associations, reported emotional involvement
in political campaigns, and had a high degree of pride
in the political system. Furthermore, through a highly
developed democratic infrastructure, citizens could
provide input through the political process and could
influence output from the administrative structure.

In contrast, Mexico represents a subject culture.
Almond and Verba refer to Mexico as a political culture
of alienation and aspiration because of its
inconsistencies and imbalances. On the one hand,
Mexicans showed the lowest frequency of political
performance. They were poorly informed about politics
and had low rates of voluntary association membership

38

and political activity. The Mexican political culture also included many persons who were alienated and parochial and who viewed their government, its bureaucracy, and the police as corrupted and insensitive to their needs. Orientations of the lower classes were toward output aspects. Expecting authority and policies to come down from the top, they did not anticipate participating in the political processes. On the other hand, Mexicans evidenced a great deal of pride in their political system. Almond and Verba attribute this[7] pride to the Mexican revolution and to the presidency. Before 1910 the Mexican political system was an exploitive one; after the revolution new norms stressed the need for political participation. These norms, however, acquired symbolic value to most Mexicans. They were preached but rarely practiced since the necessary political processes and structures did not exist. Corruption and authoritarianism persisted, and the population continued to be politically inactive. In general, to this day the vast majority of the population, especially the lower classes, have yet to accept norms of civic obligation and to develop a sense of civic competence. Most Mexicans continue to remain passive in the Mexican political culture.[8]

Contemporary Mexican social issues reflect the Mexican political culture. In discussing Mexican social and political control, Purcell (1981) discusses the secret to Mexico's political stability, despite the severity of its social problems and the increasing gap between the rich and poor. Two interlocking principles explain this stability: the first consists of mutual elite tolerance and a complex system of resolving differences among elites; the second principle is that of incorporating a relatively large percentage of the population by Latin American standards into the political system and implementing rigorous social control.

Purcell (1981) states these methods of social control have led academic observers of Mexico to label the system "authoritarian," but this term is not to be confused with "totalitarian."

> The authoritarianism of the Mexican political system is further reflected in the centralization of authority relationships. No one can contradict or criticize the president while he is in office, and that

situation is vastly different from the one in the United States. Subordinates must often refer even minor bureaucratic decisions up the hierarchy. Mexico City is the center of bureaucratic decision-making; little or nothing of importance can be decided in the provinces (Purcell, 1981:50).

Purcell (1981) asserts that while authority in Mexico to make decisions is highly centralized and hierarchical, the power to implement or not to implement decisions is often extremely decentralized. This decentralization is referred to as "mutual elite tolerance," whereby the existence of semi independent power groups within the bureaucracy and the countryside is tolerated. These are reflected in rural "caciques," where a monopoly of political and economic power is concentrated in an individual or group. The cacique is evident among Mexicans newly immigrated to the United States. Tension and conflicts result when these groups interact with Mexican-Americans who have been influenced by a participant culture and thus are not dependent on a personality or cacique for dispensing political leverage.[9]

Thus, the political cultures of Mexico and the United States differ greatly. In the United States citizens are active participants with a relatively high sense of civic competence and obligation and with an ability to influence their political system. In contrast, Mexican citizens are alienated from their political system, are passive subjects, and are oriented toward an authoritarian polity. They do not possess the degree of civic obligation and civic competence found in the United States. In Mexico subjects generally defer to their political system. Without participating in the political structure, they allow policies and administrative outputs to come from above.[10]

In countries characterized by deference to a political system, allegiance is placed more on interpersonal relations, the family, and the immediate community (i.e., the barrio) than on a centralized governmental authority.[11] Therefore one can expect that those older Hispanics born and raised in Mexico, or otherwise politically socialized to the Mexican political culture, will show political orientations characteristic of the Mexican political culture. They will probably practice a "politics of deference" in the

American political culture and will tend to be inactive participants.[12]

The extent to which the older Hispanic identifies with and is socialized to the Mexican political culture depends, of course, on the amount of time spent in the United States, his acculturation to the American political culture, and the experiences that have influenced his political attitudes and political behavior in this country and the barriers raised by the American political system. The degree to which one believes in the basic processes of American politics and is willing to participate in them (political acculturation) determines the amount of political participation in the American political culture. Acculturation is different, however, from assimilation. Assimilation implies that the members of the host society completely accept an immigrant into primary face-to-face relationships. Acculturation implies that the immigrant adopts those basic values and patterns of behavior of the host society which enable him to function effectively in the society (Gordon, 1964). Among ethnic groups acculturation can and often does take place without assimilation. Those elderly Hispanics who are first or second generation in the United States will tend to be more acculturated to American politics than recent immigrants. In general, though, most older Hispanics who identify closely with Mexico, emotionally and culturally, will have been influenced by the Mexican political culture.

The incongruency of a mixed political culture

Political cultures may or may not be congruent with the structures of the political system. Almond and Verba state that:

> ... a congruent political structure would be one appropriate for the culture: in other words, where political cognitions in the population would tend to be accurate and where affect and evaluation would tend to be favorable. In general, a parochial, subject, or participant culture would be most congruent with, respectively, a traditional political structure, a centralized authoritarian structure, and a democratic political structure. (Almond & Verba, 1963:20)

41

Thus the political culture of Mexico would be incongruent with that of the United States. When a subject political culture is mixed with a participant political culture, problems arise for those who have not been politically acculturated to the dominant political culture.[13] Thus, if a Mexican-American has been raised in or exposed to the Mexican political culture, he would not be a participant in the American political culture since he does not possess the appropriate political orientation. And if one is not an active participant in this political system, one would tend to be both alienated and powerless. In this country this appears to be the case of the older Hispanic.[14]

Evidence indicates that the older Hispanic is relatively inactive in politics. To the extent that he is inactive, his political culture is a major factor in understanding his political behavior. However, the political culture of the older Hispanic in itself does not provide a complete picture of his political experiences in this country. The theory of political culture provides the contextual framework necessary for understanding the older Hispanic persons' political orientation and its effect on their political behavior; but it does not describe the specific historical and contemporary factors which have impeded their participation in American politics. These factors, related to the incongruence of a subject political culture and a participant political culture, are revealed by examining the political socialization (both early and later life experiences), the historical developments in the age cohort, and the contemporary situation of the older Hispanic.[15]

Political Socialization

Political socialization refers to one's induction into a political culture. Through this process, a person internalizes a culture's attitudes, beliefs, cognitions, and values. It describes how

> ... a person comes to terms with the roles and norms of the concentric political worlds: local, regional, national, into which he grows up. Necessarily it focuses on formative experiences in the family, school, and primary group context that shapes ideals and gives insights into political aspects of life. (Fuchs, 1968:242)

Political socialization, however, is more than formative childhood experiences. Searing <u>et al</u>. (1973:430) state that "there is a need to examine adult socialization experiences which may mediate or even replace the role of childhood orientations." Searing <u>et al</u>. emphasize that the gap between early socialization experiences and political behavior is large. Many experiences which occur in later years can also affect a person's political attitudes and behavior. Almond and Verba feel that

> ... non-political experiences in childhood may play an important part in later political attitudes and behavior, but the impact of these experiences on politics continues throughout the adolescent and adult years. In fact, there is some evidence that later experiences have a more direct political implication. (Almond & Verba, 1963:267)

This study will assume that although early socialization experiences significantly affect an individual's basic personality predispositions and thus his political behavior, numerous other factors such as socializing agents and historical developments intervene between his earliest experiences and his later political behavior. Such political behavior as the degree of activity or involvement in politics may be best explained by examining later experiences.

Socializing agents

For Hispanics, who are now elderly, both early experiences and later ones might help explain their current political behavior and political attitudes. These experiences are products of a mixed subject-participant culture. On the one hand, older Hispanics socialized to the Mexican political culture have been affected by primary socializing agents characteristic of that culture. For example, the strong family ties in the Mexican community may have been a factor in reducing greater participation in the American political system. Gallo states that:

> ... familism, which emerges out of the social structure of an ethnic's country of origin, is internalized in the individual personality. Familism leads to an inability on the part of some ethnic groups to form any

43

kind of meaningful association outside the
nuclear family. (Gallo, 1974:20)

In the traditional Mexican family, specific roles
are assigned to the members. For example, the female
is expected to remain at home and care for the family,
and the male is expected to be the "breadwinner" and
authority figure (Heller, 1966; Paz, 1961). Most
social activities are carried out within the network of
the extended family (nuclear family and relations).
This type of family structure may have lessened the
opportunity for outside community involvement.[16]

On the other hand, other socializing agents
characteristic of the American political culture have
also affected the political orientations of the
Chicano. In the United States, certain socializing
agents (schools, church, socio-recreational groups such
as the Boy Scouts) are designed to induct individuals
into a participant political culture. These
socializing agents emphasize civic obligation and the
need to be politically aware and concerned. For some
ethnic groups, particularly Spanish speaking groups,
however, these socializing agents have had a reverse
effect. Instead of acculturating Hispanics to a
participant culture, they have reinforced subject
political orientations. The American educational
system and law enforcement agencies are two clear
examples.

In many respects the United States educational
system has been the socializing agent which has most
affected Hispanic perception of his political
environment. Until the late 1960s many Hispanic
children were formally segregated in separate buildings
or separate schools.[17] Of course, many older
Hispanics raised in Mexico did not attend school in
this country. Yet for those who did, the educational
system reinforced political orientations characteristic
of the Mexican political culture. The schools
generally did not encourage them to understand basic
American political values. Not only did very few
special civics programs encourage political
socialization, but also few programs eased the cultural
transition from the Mexican home to the American
school.[18] Teachers occupied a strategic position
for influencing Hispanic children's aspirations about
the American political process. But most teachers were
Whites who neither understood the Hispanic culture or
language nor encouraged them to participate actively in

44

American society[19] (Ulibarri, 1960; Grindley and Hentzell, 1981).

Law enforcement agencies have also been important in forming attitudes toward the United States. In effect, these agencies contributed to a prevailing culture of suspicion which created a sense of insecurity among many Hispanics. Hispanics have had prolonged and unpleasant contact with discriminatory and repressive practices of various law enforcement agencies --in particular the Texas Rangers (created to deal with the "Mexican problem"), the Border Patrol, and the United States Immigration and Naturalization Service. Hispanics naturally feared public agencies which had the powers to deport, require proof of citizenship, and otherwise threaten the citizenship and cultural status of Hispanics in this country.[20]

These examples of socializing agents are indicative of political socialization experienced by Hispanics. Socialization alone does not, however, determine a person's political attitudes, nor does it solely account for political performance. Socialization, learned ideas about politics, exposure to the political process, and reactions to all these events combine to give each person a particular, image of the society and of his role in it. In particular, later experiences and historical developments characteristic of the older person's age cohort can also reveal important events which have caused many older Hispanics to react in an alienated and subject manner. Examining the age cohorts of the Mexican- American elderly reveals that historical developments militating against participation were prevalent during their youth. As Riley et al. point out:

> The age strata within any society rests upon an historical base. Each new cohort, starting its life course at a unique point in time, has unique characteristics because of particular historical events undergone or the particular knowledge and attitudes acquired in childhood. (Riley et al., 1973:4).

If we select as our age stratum those Mexican-Americans 60 years and over and focus on the first 20 years of their lives, this would bring our focus onto the years 1903-1933. Their age cohort experience would reveal a picture of political repression, discrimination, and revolution.

The age cohort

Between 1903 and 1933 in United States and Mexican history, a series of events occurred which created an extreme amount of distrust and resentment among Whites toward Mexicans in both Mexico and the United States, especially in the rural border areas. For example, in 1910 the Mexican revolution sent to the United States a huge influx of immigrants seeking to escape the violence and chaos in Mexico. A series of "subversive" incidents in the United States were attributed to Mexicans and Chicanos; Whites viewed these incidents as an attempt by Mexicans and Chicanos to foster revolution in this country and regain the Southwest for Mexico. In the "Zimmerman" note of 1917, the Germans offered to unite Mexico and Japan with Germany in a war against the United States, to restore the Southwest to Mexico, and to give the far West to Japan. Although Mexico never considered the note seriously, it further reinforced the view that Mexicans and Mexican-Americans were not to be trusted. In addition, a variety of state laws, especially in Texas, segregated Mexicans from housing and public services. A legal system developed with overt double standards aimed primarily at controlling and subjugating Mexican-Americans. An early pattern of gerrymandering and other forms of political control were refined during this period. Poverty was extreme; illiteracy was high. Except among a handful of middle-class Mexican-Americans, political activities were practically nonexistent among Hispanics at that time (Moore, 1970). In addition, fear was further raised by the massive deportations of Mexican-Americans to Mexico, in some instances, without regard to citizenship or residency.

Within this background of distrust and violent suppression it is not surprising that Hispanics avoided any kind of political involvement, and it should not be surprising that today's elderly Hispanics exhibit behavior reflecting this formative period of their lives. Santiestevan illustrates how the older Hispanic's political behavior has been affected by his historical development.

> In the past, part of the defense against the economic, political, and social isolation imposed upon our people has been self insulation. This is particularly true of the elderly Mexican-American because he has been

rudely and cruelly used by the larger
society. The elderly Mexican-American has
withdrawn behind walls of self-protection.
He deliberately uses the differences in
language and culture to provide and emphasize
the gap between him and what he sees as a
menacing larger majority. While our young
and middle-aged Chicanos--the larger majority
of whom are native born--are on the move
demanding a piece of the action in the
mainstream of our democratic system, it is
true that a substantial number of elderly
Mexican-Americans prefer to remain safely
hidden behind their barriers. (U.S.
Congress, Senate Special Committee on Aging,
1969:430)

In summary, the political socialization and
historical development of Hispanics reveal that the
social and political environment was not conducive to
political participation. The incongruency of a subject
political culture mixed with a participant political
culture created competing forces, some characteristic
of the Mexican culture and some characteristic of the
American culture, that discouraged the development of a
sense of civic obligation and civic competence among
Hispanics. Socialization to a Mexican political
culture combined with experiences with the American
political system resulted in many older persons'
practicing a politics of deference.

The Politics of Deference

The politics of deference--used by many ethnic
groups who have faced political repression--is a stage
of political acculturation. In a study of the political and social history of Hawaii, Fuchs (1961)
details the experiences of Japanese in Hawaii, who
faced conditions similar to those encountered by
Hispanics.

In the early 1900s (1908-1924) Hawaii lacked cheap
labor. For various reasons, previous groups such as the
Chinese and Portuguese had been excluded from further
immigration. The first generation of Japanese
immigrants (Issei) brought in to work on the
plantations encountered a great deal of discrimination
and exploitation. Treated more as serfs than as hired
labor, they were beholden to the plantation foremen and
owners who held control over their jobs, their private

lives, and their ability to return to Japan. The Isseis' futile attempts to change the inhumane conditions under which they lived were confounded by their strong adherence to a traditional culture. Their traditions, reflecting a parochial political culture then existing in Japan (Ward, 1965), stressed a sense of obligation to authority: to the family, to feudal lords in Japan, and to the plantation owner in Hawaii. These traditions meant knowing one's place and keeping one's station in life. Thus, because of the complete control exercised by the Hawaiian economic hierarchy and the strong traditions which stressed obedience to authority, the Issei lived within precarious political constraints. As a result, most of the Issei and the first group of the second generation (Nissei) adopted a conservative strategy in their quest for political and social acceptance. "Conscious of place and face, they tried to adjust to the social structure, seeking acceptance within it" (Fuchs, 1961:127). Only well into the second generation and third generation (Sansei) did most Japanese throw off their policy of self-restraint and submissiveness and begin to clamor for change. The Nissei and more so the Sansei wanted to be accepted and respected as Japanese in Hawaii, no less than the Issei; but unlike the Issei, they believed that respect would have to be won through struggle against the powerful men of Hawaii rather than through deference to them. To improve their economic and political conditions on the Islands, the Nissei and Sansei eventually learned and employed American political techniques.

This brief description of the political experiences encountered by the Issei, the Nissei, and the Sansei in Hawaii provides a basis for understanding three stages of political acculturation. The first stage can be considered the "patron" (boss) stage. It is characterized by feudal societies, by the plantation system in Hawaii, and by the hacendado (landlord) system of servitude in Mexico before and after the 1910 revolution. In the patron stage, individuals have little control over their environment and depend on other parochial authorities such as the boss, foremen, or landlord for decisions that affect their private and public lives. The second stage can be termed the politics of deference. In this stage a person is no longer physically bound to a parochial authority, but because of social and economic factors is politically powerless and susceptible to exploitation and discrimination. As a result the individual allows

48

other spokesmen such as the church or state to handle political grievances. Within the politics of deference one respects hierarchy. This stage shows a need to be understood rather than a demand to be understood, and it relies on the generosity of others for positive change. It is a way of survival used by groups faced with insurmountable barriers and forced to live in politically repressive environments, as did the Chinese in nineteenth-century California, the Hispanics in the Southwest, and the Issei and Nissei of Hawaii. In effect, it buys time in the hope that barriers to full participation will soon be broken down. The final and third stage can be termed the politics of confrontation and competition. In this stage, most characteristic of a participant political culture, individuals do not acquiesce to an unfavorable political situation, but instead confront the issues and demand change. This stage is a sign of political acculturation.

A politics of deference is not an immutable, permanent stage. Even during the generation practicing it, a politics of confrontation may occur if the right conditions are present. Such conditions could conceivably include laws against discrimination, improved education, better communication with activist members of the same ethnic group, and greater positive exposure to the political system and specific political issues. For example, if these conditions were present in the Southwest, more older Hispanics would practice a politics of confrontation or competition despite past negative experiences with the political system. Whether or not these conditions are present, it might be expected that the older Hispanic, even though he has been discouraged from participation in the American political system, would at least be more receptive to Hispanic politics since contemporary Hispanics stress cultural awareness and maintenance of the Mexican heritage. It is suggested, however, by the researcher that contemporary factors such as generational conflicts and ideological disagreements have apparently created obstacles to participation by older Hispanics in Hispanic-related politics.

Contemporary Issues

Although some evidence shows that younger Hispanics feel relatively inefficacious and alienated from political involvement in this country, many have become politically acculturated to the point where they are politically active.[21] The Hispanic political movement demonstrates this. Since 1965, through such actions as voter registration drives, protest activities, and union organizing, Hispanics have become politically active. In effect, they have acquired political orientations, such as a sense of civic competence, which enable them to employ the American political system for their own benefit. Yet the political acculturation of these younger Hispanics may have also created conflict with their elders who have not achieved the same level of acculturation. These include generational conflicts and ideological disagreements.

Generational conflicts

Although data are not available to verify this, generational conflicts may militate against more active involvement by older Hispanics, particularly in Hispanic related politics. First-hand impressions lead this researcher to believe that many younger Hispanics feel that the older person is too conservative and not interested in politics. Grebler et al. refer to this when they describe the generational split:

> The classic conflict between the young and old has become more acute in the Mexican-American elite, as elsewhere ... Young Mexican-Americans, like other youth, consider themselves to be more in tune with present reality than are their elders, and so they impatiently clamor for change. Age, long a basis for authority among the Mexican-American people, is now often the target of youthful contempt. (Grebler et al., 1970:553)

With the increasing social assimilation of urban Hispanics, many traditional roles accorded the older person have disappeared. Sotomayor (1973) refers to the traditional roles of the grandparents as those of authority and decision-making, rearing of children, religious upbringing of the grandchildren, and the transmission of cultural aspects (customs, values, history, and language). With increasing urbanization among Hispanics and the subsequent breakdown of the traditional extended family, the older person may not act in some of the traditional roles he once knew. Sarinana, director of a Mexican-American senior citizen center, commented during a personal interview that many of her senior citizens felt neglected and at times

50

emotionally abused by their grandchildren involved in politics "and that it created an unfavorable impression among older Hispanics about Hispanic political activists."[22] Generational conflicts could thus be a major factor in the suspected relative inactivity of older Hispanics in Hispanic politics. If an older person feels he is not accorded proper respect or that his needs are not taken into account when other Hispanics become politically involved, he may be less willing to participate.

Ideological disagreements

Another factor related to generational conflict is the older Hispanics ideological disagreement with the goals, tactics, and philosophy of the Hispanic political movements. In the southwest, this movement expresses itself through the ideology of "Chicanismo." Chicanismo appeals for political action, economic progress, and reorientation toward a renewed cultural identity based upon common history and culture. The Chicano movement itself strongly implies that Hispanics have moved to the third stage of political acculturation and are practicing a politics of confrontation and competition, albeit nationalistic and cultural. The elderly Hispanic may perceive the ideology of the Chicano movement as detrimental to his security and position within this society. For example, if he has had negative experiences during the Mexican revolution, he may be afraid of militant action. He may be unsure of his citizenship status or may be here illegally and thus feel threatened by political action which brings his barrio to the attention of the authorities. Moreover, he may simply be grateful for what this country has done for him and thus might resent the criticism leveled by Hispanics against that same system which has apparently aided him. In all these areas ideological disagreements may affect the political attitudes and political participation by Hispanic older persons. Although concrete evidence that generational conflicts and ideological disagreements discourage older Hispanics from more active political participation does not currently exist, these factors must be taken into account in the political behavior of elderly Hispanics. They may want to be politically active, and later life experiences may have created positive attitudes toward participation. Therefore, if ideological disagreements and generational conflicts impede political participation, then these must be recognized as impediments to political involvement and interest.

Political Efficacy and Access

Political efficacy

It has been shown that the political culture of the older Hispanic may have instilled in him political orientations characteristic of a subject political culture. It has also been shown that political socialization, historical developments, and contemporary factors may have worked against the development of a sense of involvement in the American political system and Hispanic politics. In addition to a sense of involvement the older person must also feel efficacious if he is to be motivated. Political efficacy is "the feeling that individual political action does have or can have an impact upon the political process, i.e., that it is worthwhile to perform one's duties" (Conway & Feigert, 1972:42). It is the feeling that political and social change are possible and that the individual citizen can help bring this change about. Campbell et al. say that persons who feel

> ... that public officials are responsive and responsible to the electorate, who think that individual political activity is worthwhile and capable of influencing public policy, and who see that the private citizens' channels of access to governmental decision makers are not confined to the ballot box are much more likely to be politically active than those citizens who feel largely overwhelmed by the political process. (Campbell et al., 1954:194)

The sense of political efficacy has been shown to be significantly related to political participation: that is, persons who feel efficacious are much more likely to become actively involved in politics (Berelson et al., 1954; Campbell et al., 1954; Campbell et al., 1960; Dahl, 1961). Almond and Verba (1963) have also shown political efficacy to be related to political cultures with citizens of Great Britain expressing more competence in political matters than citizens of Germany, Italy, or Mexico. A widely used and well-tested scale (Robinson et al., 1968:460) consisting of four items has been developed to measure an individual's sense of political efficacy.[23]

A sense of citizen duty to participate in politics is another important political attitude relating to participation. A sense of citizen duty is defined as the feeling that all should participate in the political process, regardless of whether such political activity is seen as worthwhile or efficacious. Feelings of citizen duty are instilled by the political socialization process and have their roots in society and personality. Feeling a duty to participate seems to carry over to political action; several studies show that persons feeling a duty to participate are more likely to do so (Campbell et al., 1954; Jensen, 1960). As with political efficacy, a scale has been developed to measure an individual's sense of citizen duty (Milbrath, 1965:156).

Among Hispanics in general, a sense of political efficacy has been found to relate to their political participation. Several studies on Hispanic political participation reveal attitudes of cynicism toward political involvement in formal systems of politics. For example, among the most significant findings in the survey of Mexican-American voters in 15 Texas counties were the low efficacy and high alienation levels. Table 7 (McCleskey & Merrill, 1973:795) shows that Hispanics exhibit a lower sense of efficacy than Whites and a higher sense of alienation than Whites. The authors attribute the high cynicism among Texas Hispanics and Blacks to the Whites' domination of the Texas political system.

Access

In addition to a sense of involvement and a sense of efficacy, the older person must have access to the political arena. Access is concerned with legal, physical, social, and environmental barriers to participation such as health, income, education, and tenure of residence. Of immediate concern for the older person is that his basic physical needs be met. Without sufficient food, good health, and an adequate income to buy necessities, the older person will not be able to concern himself with politics. Maslow's motivational theory (1954) refers to a hierarchy of needs considered important for human behavior. These needs include physical necessities, safety or security, belongingness, self-esteem, and self-actualization. As part of his theory Maslow points out that physical needs such as food and water must first be satisfied. If these basic needs are neglected, people will

TABLE 7

POLITICAL EFFICACY AND POLITICAL ALIENATION
AMONG TEXAS VOTERS, BY RACE AND ETHNICITY
(Percentage)

	Anglo (N=797)	Negro (N=419)	Hispanic (N=305)
Degree of efficacy			
High	24	8	10
Medium	49	46	46
Low	27	46	44
Political alienation			
High	25	52	36
Medium	30	34	38
Low	45	14	26

SOURCE: McCleskey and Merrill (1973:795).

apathetically turn away from politics as a consequence of their intense preoccupation with survival (Davies, 1963). A person who must concentrate all his energies on staying alive cannot concern himself actively or passively with politics. Sufficient income is closely associated with the ability to meet basic needs. Studies in many Western countries show that income is positively correlated with political participation (Agger & Ostrom, 1965; Campbell et al., 1954; Tingsten, 1937; Lane, 1959). Physical health is also important to the fulfillment of basic needs. Because of the degenerative effects of advancing age, older persons are more likely to be inactive politically if they are ill or physically disabled.

Also related to access, but beyond basic needs, are education, sex, legal status (citizenship), mobility, and geographical location. In many Western countries those with higher education are more likely to participate in politics (Agger & Goldrich, 1958; Almond & Verba, 1963; Dahl, 1961; Woodward & Roper, 1950). The five-nation study shows that educational differences more significantly accounted for differences in participation in Italy, Germany, and Mexico than in the United Kingdom and the United States (Almond & Verba, 1963). In terms of political participation, sex is still found to be an important factor. Many studies have shown that men are more likely to participate in politics than are women (Agger et al., 1964; Almond & Verba, 1963; Berelson et al., 1954; Lane, 1959; Buchanon, 1956).

Eligibility rules and citizenship status can directly affect the ability and willingness of persons, especially ethnic group members, to participate in political activities. In many cases, non-English speaking groups have been excluded from voting by language requirements (Grebler et al., 1970), while other groups have been excluded through such requirements as poll taxes and residency require-ments.24 The lack of transportation can prevent an individual from participating, especially in rural areas where distances are great or in urban areas where public transportation is inadequate. Whether an individual originally comes from a rural or urban area can affect his rate of political participation (Rowan, 1973). Generally, those from urban areas are more likely to participate than those from rural areas (Campbell, 1962). The size of the community also relates to political participation. Generally, the larger the community the higher the rate of participation. Metropolitan areas have the highest participation rates, smaller cities and towns are next, and rural areas have the lowest rates (Campbell et al., 1960; Campbell & Kahn, 1952).

It is expected that the older Hispanic will feel inefficacious and will not have as much access to participation as Hispanics in general and the White elderly. The effects of a subject-participant political culture, political socialization experiences, historical developments, and contemporary factors will all contribute to a feeling of inefficacy. The older Hispanic will also have greater difficulties maintaining access because his old age, low socio-economic status, and uncertain citizenship make him more susceptible to legal, social, economic, and physical barriers to participation.

An Overview of Factors Related to Political Activity

Any examination of the relative importance of socialization, historical developments, and contemporary issues to the older Hispanic's political behavior should include a diagram of the various factors that may influence his political attitudes and political participation. Model A (Fig. 1) shows that the overriding factor in the older person's political orientation is the effect of a mixed subject-participant political culture: Mexico and the United States. The Mexican political culture has instilled in the older Hispanic subject political orientations, incongruent with the American political culture. This mix leads to socializing agents which discourage political participation and further reinforce subject political orientations. Combined with this incongruency, and partly a result (shown by dotted lines) of it, are historical events which further discourage political participation. Continued political inactivity and political alienation are currently fostered by a combination of contemporary issues and access features such as generational conflicts and low socioeconomic status. The final result of these factors illustrated in the diagram is a politics of deference manifested in political inactivity and political alienation.

Certainly not all older Hispanics are politically inactive or practice a politics of deference, nor are

56

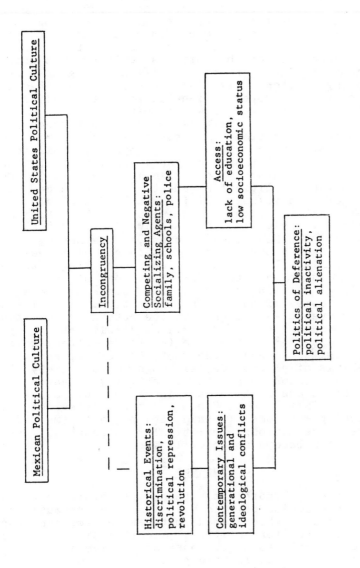

Fig. 1.--Model A.

all older Hispanics affected by these factors to the same degree or in the same combination. The diagram merely shows the relationship of these factors to each other and to current political behavior and suggests possibilities that may occur in certain situations. Some older persons will be found to be politically active regardless of the political culture into which they were socialized or the socializing agents and contemporary factors with which they may have had to deal. As has been noted, alienation from the political system is correlated with low participation. But this is not always so. Political researchers generally assume that alienation and estrangement from the political structure leads to apathy, political withdrawal, and a low level of participation. But the politically alienated might also be swept up in the enthusiasm for a political movement. For instance, in periods of political crisis extraordinarily high political participation often occurs. The Mexican Revolution of 1910 is one example of this.[25] Individuals who had been cynical, apathetic, or apolitical are capable under certain circumstances of becoming politically active and opposing those conditions which created their feelings of cynicism. Model B (Fig. 2) (Yinger, 1973:186) diagrams several possible outcomes of anomie and alienation. The pluses (+) and minuses (-) assigned to the return arrows show that the consequences of anomie and alienation can either increase (+) or decrease (-) those factors which caused them to occur. One must, therefore, remember that feelings of alienation, although most likely to decrease a person's political activity, can under certain conditions lead to an increase in political activity. This model has direct relevance to understanding why some Hispanics and perhaps some older Hispanics, even though politically alienated, have become and can become politically active.

Conclusions

A general hypothesis, then, is this: that the older Hispanic is politically inactive because of various factors which impede motivation necessary for participation and for political acculturation. These factors contribute to a low sense of involvement in the political system and Hispanic politics and to a feeling of political inefficacy.

The theory of political culture suggests that older Hispanics socialized to the Mexican political

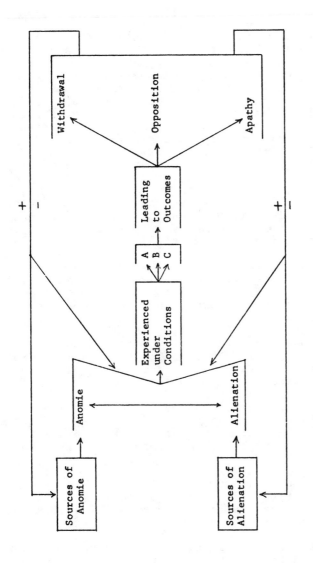

Fig. 2.--Model B.

culture are likely to possess political orientations incongruent with the American political culture. These political orientations in conjunction with socializing agents such as the American education system, may contribute to a politics of deference characteristic of persons socialized to the Mexican political culture. The politics of deference appears as a sense of alienation from politics and can be compounded by the political socialization and historical developments older Hispanics have experienced in this country. Discrimination, revolution, and political repression evident in their age cohort combine to lessen the chances that the older Hispanic will have either a sense of involvement in politics or a sense of efficacy. Therefore, further hypotheses emerge:

1. That because of their social, economic, cultural, and political position, the elderly Hispanic will be found to cluster near the low end of a hierarchy of political involvement (apathetic, least active).

2. That those who rank low in a sense of political efficacy and citizen duty will be politically alienated and will show such alienation through low rates of political participation.

3. That those with negative experiences in politics during their lifetimes will express negative feelings about participation in politics.

Because of generational conflicts and ideological disagreement which may serve to discourage political activity, participation in Hispanic related politics is probably not high. Therefore it is further hypothesized:

4. That because of discouragement (generational conflicts) by younger Hispanics, the level of participation in Hispanic politics for older Hispanics will be low.

5. That because of ideological disagreement with Hispanic political strategies older Hispanics will express negative attitudes toward Hispanic politics.

Many older Hispanics are probably active in politics. They have probably experienced certain events which altered their political attitudes and gave them a sense of involvement and efficacy. To determine why these older persons are active, the study will control for the politically active respondent and will examine the characteristics of this subgroup.

Summary

This chapter has explored reasons for the suspected political inactivity among older Hispanics. Through a review of the literature of political science and the use of Almond and Verba's theory of political culture, various factors were cited which might account for political inactivity among older Hispanics in this country. An important cultural factor is that the older Hispanic did not grow up in an environment which motivated him to participate. Almond and Verba's theory of political culture suggests that Hispanics socialized to the Mexican political culture were instilled with political orientations different from those of the American political culture. Mexico is characterized by a citizenry alienated from its political system, whereas the United States is characterized by active participants who have a sense of civic obligation and civic competence. Therefore, those older Hispanics raised in Mexico or otherwise socialized to the Mexican political culture can be expected to practice a politics of deference, characteristic of a subject political culture. In addition, other factors may impede participation and political acculturation in the American political culture. These factors include political socialization experiences and historical developments occurring during the older person's lifetime. These experiences partly result from the incongruence between a subject culture and a participant culture. On the one hand, the older Hispanic has been affected by socializing agents such as strong family bonds which lessen allegiance to a centralized authority. On the other hand, he has been affected by other socializing agents such as the educational system, which were supposedly designed to acculturate ethnic groups to American politics, but which actually discouraged political acculturation. In addition, the age cohort of older Hispanics indicates discrimination and political repression, which further encourage the older persons' cynicism and insecurity about participation in politics.

Contemporary factors also form important reasons why the older Hispanic may not be motivated to participate in politics, particularly Hispanic related politics. Ideological disagreements and generational conflicts are suggested as reasons for low participation in Hispanic related politics. In addition, access to participation by older Hispanics is probably more difficult than that for White elderly and Hispanics in general because of the older person's low socioeconomic status and citizenship problems. As a result of the above factors, the older Hispanic may not be sufficiently motivated to participate because he feels he has no stake in the political system or in Hispanic politics, because he feels inefficacious, and because he probably does not have as great an access to political participation as the White elderly and Hispanics in general.

Footnotes -- Chapter II

1. A third level of politics exists which is referred to as "subsystem politics": a focus on particular functional areas of activity (i.e., airline regulations) which involves interrelationships among congressional committees, administrative agencies (or bureaus), and interest groups (Anderson, p. 48, 1979).

2. Verba (1965) states that the term "political culture" was first used in Gabriel Almond "Comparative Political Systems," Journal of Politics 18 (1956).

3. Orientation refers to internalized aspects of objects and relationships. It includes (1) "cognitive orientations," knowledge of and beliefs about the political system, its roles, and the incumbents of these roles, its inputs and its objects; (2) "affective orientation," or feelings about the political system, its roles, personnel, and performance; and (3) "evaluational orientation," the judgments and opinions about political objects that typically involve the combination of value standards and criteria with information and feelings (Almond and Verba, 1963:14).

4. The participant political culture can also be considered a civic culture. The civic culture is defined as a participant political culture in which the political culture and the political structures are congruent. Individuals are oriented not only to political inputs, but also to the input process. The individual not only is an active participant, but supports both the political structure and process of the political system (Almond & Verba, 1963).

5. This is a familiar and contemporary problem in western political cultures. This type of culture has been the case for France, Germany, and Italy during the nineteenth and twentieth centuries. Almond and Verba state that a "successful shift from a subject to a participant culture involves the diffusion of positive orientations toward a democratic infrastructure, the acceptance of norms of civic obligation, and the development of a sense of civic competence among a substantial proportion of the population" (1963:27).

6. The characteristics of the political culture of Mexico is also useful for understanding the political behavior of Mexican immigrants and

undocumented aliens who have resided in the United States over long periods of time without assimilating or moving out of ethnic enclaves.

7. The presidency refers to the office of the president as the chief executive position in the Mexican government. The individual holding that office is considered to be the symbol of Mexican national unity.

8. Scott (1965) describes the Mexican political system as a subject political culture. He argues that most Mexicans are characterized by both strong dependency needs and by rejective and rebellious tendencies. This ambivalence, according to Scott, pervades the family, school, work group, and governmental political system. Scott also points out that Mexico is not a homogeneous political culture. Although he, Pye and Verba (1965), and Almond and Verba (1963) characterize Mexico as a subject culture, Scott estimates that at present Mexico's political culture includes 25 percent parochials, all in the popular or lowest sector; of these one-third are Indians. Approximately 10 percent are participants, found primarily in the upper and in the stable middle class; and of these not more than 1 or 2 percent can be characterized as viewing politics from the perspective of the democratic "civic culture." The remaining 65 percent, who are considered subjects, include 15 percent of the popular class, 20 percent of a transitional group (those moving from the lower to the middle class), most of the marginal middle class, many of the stable class, and even a few from the upper class.

9. Novak (1982) carries this thesis to a political economic level when he argues that social and cultural factors such as these have been largely responsible for poverty in Latin America and not, as marxists claim, American capitalism. He ascribes this to the Latin Catholic theology which historically accumulated and controlled wealth and power and stifled private initiative, property and capital This system was transferred to the Latin American colonies where it is now reflected in certain values such as aristocratic ethic, luck, and personal personages, which contrast to North American values of diligence, regularity and initiative.

10. Italy has a political culture similar to Mexico's but different in several respects. It is characterized as an alienated political culture. Almond and Verba's survey found that the political culture is characterized by relatively unrelieved political alienation, social isolation, and apathy. The Italians rated low in national pride and in a sense of civic obligation and civic competence to join with others in situations of political stress. In general, Italians possessed neither allegiance to their culture nor allegiance to political participation. In this country, more than in others, the primary social unit was the family which in large measure contributed to the distrust and alienation exhibited toward the central government and the political process. Gallo (1974) also found many of these same characteristics, including the overall importance of the family in politics.

11. In a study of a village in southern Italy Banfield (1958) characterized the political culture of the area as "amoral familism." This culture accords legitimacy neither to the central government nor to civic-political organs of party, interest group, or local community.

12. The politics of deference refers to individuals who defer to the political system rather than compete or participate. In many cases they are forced to defer because a repressive, exploitive atmosphere exists, making political participation risky. The theory of the politics of deference, developed in part by Lawrence Fuchs of Brandeis University, is further elaborated later in this chapter.

13. Almond and Verba do not view the political culture of the United States as a mixed one. They feel this country has already gone through that stage and is now a homogeneous culture. However, in their analysis of the American political culture they did not examine the political situation of Hispanics. Therefore, I have taken the liberty of classifying the Hispanic political situation in this country as being that of a mixed political culture.

14. Purcell (1981) in discussing the problems between Mexico and the United States and in framing the reasons for the continued severity of Mexico's social problems suggests that an important beginning to

framing the policy debates is to attack the root of
mutual Mexican and United States misperceptions about
the nature of each others social processes. He states
that United States perceptions of society "rest on
assumptions about a fluid and relatively homogeneous
(except racially) social structure characterized by
individual mobility, self-help, political pluralism,
and an emphasis on the future rather than the past"
(p. 54). The equivalent Mexican assumptions (which
North Americans sometimes mistake for variations of
"marxism") emphasize "major structural and social
inequalities, social forces or classes rather than
individuals, historical processes, and a close
connection between state and society and between polity
and economy" (p. 54).

15. Incongruency affects younger age segments of
the Hispanic populations. In examining the status of
young Hispanics, studies have characterized their
"marginal" situation as being neither fully
acculturated into the American social and political
system or fully assimilated into Mexican traditions.
In southwestern cities the "zoot suit" pachucos of the
1940's and the low riders of the 1980's exemplify the
marginality of many Hispanic youth who retain Mexican
characteristics, although born and raised in this
country, but do not have the educational or cultural
values of United States society which enable them to
function effectively.

16. In general, this type of traditional family
structure appears to be declining in some areas of the
Southwest (Moore, 1970).

17. Although this practice is not now prevalent,
most schools attended by Hispanics are still located in
the poorest areas and thus largely segregated on a de
facto basis.

18. For further discussion of the problems of
Mexican-American education see Brown, Rosen, Hill, and
Olivas, The Condition of Education for Hispanic
Americans. National Center for Education Statistics,
Washington, D.C., 1980.

19. For a detailed and sensitive view of the
growing Hispanic population in California and their
present and future impact see the symposia conducted by
SRI International (Grindley and Hentzell, 1981). The
symposia brought together 100 representatives from

community groups, local government, and the business and corporate world to discuss the efforts needed to involve Hispanics in developing an effective and economically strong future for California.

20. For a detailed and incisive treatment of Hispanic-police relations see Robert Derbyshire, "Children's Perceptions of the Police: A Comparative Study of Attitudes and Attitude Change," pp. 175-183; Armando Morales, "Chicano-Police Riots," pp. 184-202, both in Chicano: Social and Psychological Perspectives, ed. Nathaniel Wagner and Marsha Haug (St. Louis, Mo.: C.V. Mosby Co., 1971); Ruben Sandoval and Douglas Martinez. "Police Brutality -- the New Epidemic," Agenda: September/October, 1978; and Rudolfo Acuna, Occupied America: A History of Chicanos (2nd ed.) Harper and Row: New York, 1981.

21. This is indicated in a survey of the political orientations of Hispanic children (Garcia, 1974). In a measure of attitudes which favorably predispose a person to participate in political activities, the survey indicated that the Mexican-American ranked lower than the Anglo-American child. The study concluded that the psychological support conducive to future participation in electoral politics is relatively low among contemporary Mexican-American youth.

22. An interview with Ramona Sarinana, director of the Libertad Senior Citizen Center, during the spring of 1973.

23. For a comprehensive listing of scales and measures of political attitudes see John Robinson, J. Rush, and K. Head, Measures of Political Attitudes. (Ann Arbor: Survey Research Center, University of Michigan, 1968).

24. Until a court decision (Castro vs. California, 1970) overruled the applicable section of California's election code, it had disfranchised all but those literate in English.

25. Scott (1965:339) cites Levy's observation (see Marion Levy, "A Philosopher's Stone," World Politics 5, July 1953:555-68) that a surprising number of members of the lower class traditional group participated in the Mexican Revolution of 1910, a very few as leaders but many more as fighters.

Chapter III

ANALYSIS OF STUDY FINDINGS

Introduction

The elderly Hispanic may be politically inactive for a variety of reasons. For example, he has grown up in a political environment formed by two incongruent political cultures. Socialization to a subject political culture, negative socializing agents from a participant political culture and historical events may have discouraged his political participation and reinforced his subject political orientations. In addition, contemporary factors such as generational conflicts, ideological disagreements, and problems with access to the political arena may have impeded participation and may have created negative attitudes toward Hispanic politics and age related activities. This chapter will examine these issues as they pertain to the basic question: what is the extent and nature of political participation among the Hispanic elderly?

Specifically, this chapter will describe the research study and will examine the political attitudes and the rate of political activity of the sample: Part I provides a composite picture of the sample through profiles on socioeconomic status, family structure, and ethnic makeup; Part II provides rates of political activity according to six dimensions of political and social participation; and Part III describes attitudes toward Hispanic politics, senior citizen affairs, and the sociopolitical status of the Hispanic elderly.

Study group

The sample consists of 106 randomly selected elderly Hispanics ranging in age from 50 to 90 years. The original plan called for interviewing only males, since it was thought the female would be inactive for traditional reasons. However, the pretesting revealed that the female was often as active as, and in some cases more active than, the male. Thus, the interviews included both males and females.

The respondents live in the Hispanic barrios of San Jose, California. The survey area is identified as

69

the San Jose target area by The Aging Population of Santa Clara County: A Study (1973). In this county the study identifies seven target areas marked by high concentrations of older persons having low incomes and other socioeconomic characteristics indicating potential need for social services. The combined target areas encompass nearly 50 percent of all Spanish Surname/Spanish Language (SS/SL) older persons in the entire county. The study specifically focused on the San Jose target areas. Of the 4,489 older persons (SS/SL) in the target areas, 3,102 or 63 percent live in the San Jose target area. The San Jose target area is composed of East San Jose and part of the downtown area. It includes 25 contiguous census tracts accounting for a population of 160,000, or nearly one-fourth of the city's total population (657,600).

Method

The study employed a two-stage cluster sample. According to Mendenhall et al., this sample "is obtained by first selecting a simple random sample of clusters and then selecting a simple random sample of elements from each sampled cluster" (Mendenhall et al., 1971:171). As he states,

> two stage cluster sampling is advantageous when a frame listing all elements in the population is not available or when it is desirable to have sample elements in geographic proximity because of travel costs. (Mendenhall et al., 1971:172)

In the survey 10 census tracts were selected at random from the 25 census tracts within the San Jose target area. Each census tract was assigned a quota of 10 older Hispanics to be interviewed. Within each census tract a sample of five blocks was randomly chosen from which two older Hispanics were interviewed for each block. Because this procedure obviated enumeration, allowed the interviewer to work in a given place for a specified time, and thereby reduced travel time, it was an efficient method for conducting the survey.

At the outset of the survey it became time consuming and at times difficult to locate the older person within a given block. However, early in the survey, the researcher was fortunate to meet a local mailman who was able to pinpoint , for a particular

block, where each older Hispanic lived.   Through   most
of the survey, mailmen identified where older Hispanics
resided   and   thus   saved   considerable   time   for   the
researcher.

Data Collection

The questionnaire

Primary   data   were   collected   in   a   structured
questionnaire   which   was   designed to yield information
on the following   areas   (for   a   description   of   the
research   design   and   factors   affecting research with
elder Hispanics see Appendix A):

1. Socioeconomic profile-age, income, occupation,
    education.

2. Political   participation-type   of   activities,
    frequency of activities.

3. Awareness index-knowledge of political issues,
    leaders, and organizations.

4. Indices   of   political   efficacy   and   citizen
    duty.

5. Attitudes-projective   tests,   open-ended
    questions.

6. Political   socialization-historical   develop-
    ments, personal experiences.

Dependent variables

The   study   utilized   a   set   of   dependent   and
independent   variables   which   served   to   organize the
questions and the analysis.   The   dependent   variable,
which   are   each   multivariate,   consist   of social and
political   indicators   of   participation.   The   primary
dependent   variable is political participation. The six
separate variables describing this   primary   dependent
variable concern six dimensions of political and social
participation.   As   a   guide   to   the   discussion   of
dimensions which constitute dependent variables,   refer
to   the   outline   below   (see   Appendix   A for detailed
description of each variable).

71

Dimensions of Political and Social Participation

I. Political Participation
   A. Political Awareness
      1. Familiarity of leaders and organizations
      2. Support of leaders and organizations
      3. Discussion of politics and public problems
   B. Membership in Formal Organizations
      1. Membership in unions
      2. Membership in political groups
      3. Membership in civic groups
   C. Voting Behavior
      1. Registration to vote
      2. Total vote frequency
   D. Past Political Activities
      1. Hispanic related politics
      2. Old-age related politics
      3. General citizenship

II. Social Participation
   A. Religious Activity
      1. Membership in church
      2. Membership in religious organizations
   B. Senior Citizen Activity
      1. Membership in senior clubs

Independent variables

Like the dependent variables, the independent variables are multivariate, consisting of attitudes, correlates, and factors which affect political participation. In contrast to the dependent variables, the independent variables are more complex. These independent variables include (for detailed description see Appendix A):

1. Political efficacy and sense of citizen duty
2. Political socialization (historical development)
3. Ethnic identification
4. Generational conflicts and ideological disagreements
5. Socioeconomic status and functional ability
6. Attitudes

Part I: Profiles

To draw a composite picture of the sample, information was collected on several dimensions—socioeconomic status, family structure, and ethnic

72

identification. The profiles describe the characteristics of this group and provide an important background for examining political behavior since the information concerns an understudied and a unique subgroup of the Hispanic population.

Socioeconomic status

Of the 106 respondents, 51 were male and 55 were females, wih ages ranging from 52 to 88. The largest group, 29 percent, were between 61 and 65 (Table 8).[1]

TABLE 8[a]

AGE OF RESPONDENTS
(N=106)

	50-55	56-60	61-65	66-70	71-75	76-80	Over 80
Number	5	8	31	22	21	4	15
Percentage	5	8	29	21	20	4	14

[a] Because of rounding to the nearest whole percentage, total percentages in various tables throughout Chapters III, IV, and V may be equal to, less than, or more than 100 percent.

By national standards (in 1975), the income of approximately 40 percent of this sample falls close to the poverty line.[2] Fifty-six percent received less than $4,000 a year, 40 percent received less than $3,000 a year, and 19 percent recieved between $6,000 and $10,000 (see Table 9). No one in this sample earned more than $10,000. The primary source of income is Social Security, with some Old Age and Survivors Disability Insurance (OASDI) assistance. Because of the Supplemental Security Income (SSI) Act, recipients are ineligible for food stamps. The lack of sufficient funds to purchase food, transportation, clothing, and other basic necessities forces some of the respondents to rely on their children for supplemental income.

TABLE 9

INCOME OF RESPONDENTS
(N=98)

Income	Number	Percentage
$1,000-1,999	4	4
$2,000-2,999	35	36
$3,000-3,999	16	16
$4,000-4,999	16	16
$5,000-5,999	8	8
$6,000-6,999	15	15
$7,000-10,000	4	4

Because many of the respondents have been poor most of their lives, their current poverty is not new to them. Of the 94 respondents who answered a question about their past financial condition, 44 (47 percent) stated that they had been poor to very poor most of their lives; 27 (29 percent) had been poor but able to live comfortably; and 23 (24 percent) stated that they had been fairly well off (middle income) most of their lives.

The most frequently stated past occupations were housewife (33 percent), employment in canneries, sheds, or packing houses which predominate in the Santa Clara Valley (22 percent), and farmwork (20 percent).[3] Twenty-five percent had worked in various other occupations: in construction, as mechanics, and in unskilled labor jobs (car wash, janitors). It had been anticipated that most of the Hispanic elderly would have farmworkers' background; that most did not could be attributed to the fact that many Hispanics in the Santa Clara Valley turned to the fruit and vegetable canneries instead of remaining in the "migrant stream."[4] Only 12 (11 percent) of the total sample are currently employed.

The data show little formal education: 51 (48 percent) received one to six years of education, and 26 (25 percent) received no education. However, 28 (26 percent) received seven to 12 years, and one respondent had some college education.

Family structure

Among the 105 respondents who indicated their marital status, 68 (65 percent) were married, 29 (28 percent) were widowed, two (2 percent) were divorced, and only two (2 percent) were single. The remaining four respondents were separated from their spouses. Compared to the national norm, this group was characterized by large families. Forty-five percent had five children or more and only 6 percent had no children (see Table 10). Most of the children lived in San Jose or within the county. Sixty-five percent of the children saw their parents regularly (at least weekly). However, most of the respondents lived alone or with spouses. Of the total sample, 70 (66 percent) reported that no children lived with them and only 16 (15 percent) reported living with other relatives. Only 16 (15 percent) of the respondents had parents who were living. Among these respondents, 12 reported that their parents were living in the United States.

TABLE 10

CHILDREN OF RESPONDENTS
(N=105)

Number of Children	Number	Percentage
0	6	6
1-2	24	23
3-4	27	26
5-6	19	18
7-8	15	14
9+	14	13

Ethnic identification

Of the 106 respondents, 45 (42 percent) were born in the United States and 61 (58 percent) were born in Mexico. Of those born in the United States, the largest number, 18, were born in Texas, 10 were born in New Mexico, four were born in California, and 13 in other states. Although the respondents were born in

75

states as far away as Illinois, 36 (80 percent) of those born in the United States were born in the border states of Texas, New Mexico, and Arizona.

A majority of the respondents were not only born in Mexico but were also raised there. Sixty-three (59 percent) were raised in Mexico; two of the American-born respondents returned to Mexico to be raised. Even today, this is not uncommon in the border states. Because most of the respondents were born in the border states or in Mexico, a majority of them had a close association with the Mexican political culture during the formative periods of their lives.

Since Hispanics have only recently been an urban population, it had been assumed that a large majority of the sample would have been raised in a rural area; however, only 56 (53 percent) reported having been raised in rural areas.[5] One possible explanation for the high number of persons raised in urban areas is that many of the persons were born and raised in urban areas of Mexico.

Citizenship is one important indicator of allegiance to Mexico because maintaining Mexican citizenship may indicate resistance to severing Mexican ties or it may indicate the complication of obtaining American citizenship. Among the sample 40 (38 percent) were still citizens of Mexico, whereas 66 (62 percent) were citizens of the United States. Since arrival in the United States, 21 respondents have become citizens. Of those born in Mexico, over half (64 percent) came to the United States by 1930; the most recent period of arrival to the United States, 1950-1960, was well over 20 years ago (see Table 11). This suggests that a long period existed in which citizenship could have been obtained. Of those who did become citizens, 59 percent took six or more years to obtain their citizenship papers (see Table 12). In general, the respondents attributed the lack of citizenship to procedural barriers. When asked why they were not citizens of the United States, of 17 who responded to this delicate question, the largest number, 13, said they had not done so because they did not speak English, could not read or write, or did not know the procedures necessary to become a citizen.

Another indicator of allegiance to Mexico is the frequency with which Mexico is visited by the respondents. Eight visited Mexico at least yearly, 19

TABLE 11
YEAR OF ARRIVAL IN THE UNITED STATES
(N=59)

Year	Number	Percentage
1884–1910	3	5
1911–1920	25	42
1921–1930	10	17
1931–1940	6	10
1941–1950	9	15
1951–1960	6	10

TABLE 12
TIME IN THE UNITED STATES BEFORE BECOMING A CITIZEN
(N=22)

Time	Number	Percentage
1 year	0	0
2–3 years	3	14
4–5 years	6	27
6–10 years	7	32
11 or more years	6	27

at least every other year, and 55 rarely or never
visited Mexico. The remainder of the total sample did
not indicate whether they visited Mexico.

Although actual figures were not obtained on the
number who knew only Spanish and those who were
bilingual, approximately half of the sample knew
English, but most preferred to speak Spanish.

Summary

The sample population is characterized as poor,
uneducated, and unskilled. When their socioeconomic
position is compared to that of the general elderly
population in Santa Clara County, the White aged, and
the total Hispanic population, the results are
striking. However, this sample's socioeconomic status
is representative of that of the Spanish speaking
elderly population at the time the data was obtained.
For example, the population report of 1971 indicate
that the median income for all Spanish-surname
Americans 65 years and over was \$3,756,[6] while the
median income for this sample of Hispanic aged is
\$3,250. The median income for all Hispanics at that
time was \$5,488.[7] In sharp contrast, the median
income for all householders at that same period in
Santa Clara County was \$11,150,[8] while for the White
aged it was \$5,600.[8] Clearly, the Hispanic aged
are the most economically deprived of all these
groups.

Historically, the Hispanic elderly have depended
on extended family relationships, but increased
urbanization has weakened family networks. This
sample's data suggest that the family structures remain
basically intact, but that a sense of isolation also
exists. For example, the frequency of contact between
children and their parents would lead one to support
the notion of the maintenance of strong family ties.
However, many of the elderly Hispanicsexpressed a sense
of isolation and abandonment, which they attributed to
infrequent visits from their grandchildren, who were
also poor and too busy with their own lives to spend
much time with the grandparents. Some felt neglected,
while others thought that their children were becoming
assimilated and unappreciative of the older person.

The data on ethnic identification implied that the
sample maintains a strong attachment to Mexico.
Fifty-nine percent of the sample were raised in

Mexico. Forty of the respondents are still citizens of Mexico, while 27 respondents visit that country at least every other year. In addition, most of the respondents prefer to speak Spanish.

Part II: Rates of Political Activity

One purpose of the study is to determine the level of political interests and political participation among the Hispanic aged in the sample. Four areas of political involvement analyzed are political awareness, membership in formal organizations, voting behavior, and past political activities. In addition, the study analyzes social involvement: church activities and senior citizen centers. These six areas constitute the dependent variables of political participation. This section will examine the rates of activity in the areas of participation and will compare the rates of activity to those of the White aged and Hispanics in general.

Political awareness

Because Hispanic leaders and organizations have in recent years been highly visible in the San Jose barrios, familiarity with well-known Hispanic leaders and with major Hispanic organizations, support of the Hispanic leaders and organizations, and political interests were used as measures of awareness. The leaders and organizations chosen reflect various political ideologies (conservative, liberal, militant); thus, a measurement of awareness indicates the types of leaders and organizations the elderly Hispanics were most likely to be familiar with and support. The questionnaire mentioned the following organizations and leaders:

1. GI Forum--a conservative to moderate middle-class organization.

2. Mexican-American Political Association (MAPA)--a liberal Hispanic political association.

3. La Raza Unida Party--a militant Hispanic political third party.

4. UFW--an activist farmworkers' union.

5. La Confederacion-an activist San Jose coalition of grass-roots organizations.

79

6. Libertad Center--an Hispanic senior center in the East Side.

7. Corky Gonzalez--a militant urban Hispanic leader from Denver.

8. Cesar Chavez--a leader of the farmworkers' union.

9. Angel Gutierrez--founder of La Raza Unida party (from Texas).

10. Ernest Abeytia--a San Jose Hispanic community leader.

11. Al Garza--an Hispanic councilman.

12. Ramona Sarinana--director of the Libertad Center.

The two most familiar organizations were the UFW (50) and the Libertad Center (23); the two least familiar organizations were MAPA (six) and the Confederacion (nine).[9] Chavez and Sarinana, associated with the two most familiar organizations, were also the most familiar to the respondents. Chavez had the highest familiarity rating (67), with Sarinana second highest (30). The two local leaders Abeytia and Garza, were also well known (23 and 24 respectively). The two persons with the lowest familiarity rating were Gonzalez (six) and Gutierrez (seven). Their geographical distance and their association with militant organizations can, in part, explain their low familiarity rating. In general, the respondents displayed familiarity with the various leaders and organizations.

In addition to seeking the level of familiarity with these political leaders and organizations, the questioning probed whether the respondents who expressed familiarity also supported (were in agreement with the goals and actions of) the organizations. In general, the support ratings paralleled the familiarity ratings. The UFW and the Libertad Center and their leaders, Chavez and Sarinana, had the greatest support, whereas La Raza Unida Party and La Confederacion had the least support. Gutierrez and Gonzalez, militant leaders of the two latter organizations, also received the least support.

The UFW and the Libertad Center received the greatest familiarity and support among the respondents. Two possible reasons for this are: (1) one-fifth of the respondents come from a farmworker background and understand the problems of the UFW, and (2) the Libertad Center is directly involved with issues concerning older Hispanics in San Jose. Conversations with the respondents who were familiar with the various leaders and organizations suggest that the ideology of these leaders and organizations may not be of primary importance to the Hispanic elderly. Instead, support for these groups and individuals may depend more on the perceived significance these groups and individuals have for the elderly.

Political interest was measured by the frequency of discussion about politics or public problems with other community members. As Table 13 shows, more respondents talk about politics with their friends (51 percent) and neighbors (49 percent) than with their family (36 percent) or priest (24 percent). Older persons were least likely to have discussions with community leaders, government bureaucrats, and public officials.

Comparing this sample to an Hispanic sample of all age groups in Nebraska reveals that frequency of discussion with others is similar in each category except neighbors and family. The San Jose sample discussed politics less often with family but more often with neighbors.

Membership in organizations

Membership in formal organizations is low among members of the sample. Three respondents are active (attend regularly) members of a civic group (primarily GI Forum and a women's club), and five are active members of a political group (Model Cities and MAPA).[10]   Unions have no active members among this sample. When compared to the White aged and the sample of Hispanics from Nebraska, this sample rates favorably in terms of membership in political groups but rates low in civic group membership (see Table 14).

TABLE 13

COMPARISON OF POLITICAL DISCUSSIONS BETWEEN
THE SAN JOSE
SAMPLE AND A NEBRASKA SAMPLE OF CHICANOS OF ALL AGES

Discussion of Politics and Public Problems with	San Jose Sample			Nebraska Sample	
	N	No	Yes	N	Yes
Family	103	64%	36%	156-177[a]	69%
Friends	104	49%	51%		56%
Neighbors	103	51%	49%		21%
Priest	102	76%	24%		27%
Community leader	102	80%	20%		19%
Bureaucrat	101	94%	6%		8%
Officials	101	89%	11%		14%

[a]Welch et al. (1973:803).

82

TABLE 14

MEMBERSHIP IN CIVIC AND POLITICAL GROUPS
(Percentage)

Group	White Population[a] 55 and Over	San Jose Hispanics 50 and Over	Nebraska Hispanics[b] All Age Groups
Civic	20	3	--
Political	5	5	9

[a] Hausknecht (1962:85)

[b] Welch et al. (1973:804)

Voting behavior

Thirty-nine (37 percent) of the sample are currently registered to vote. Among the 67 (63 percent) not registered, 27 gave lack of citizenship as the main reason. Another 17 cited illiteracy and confusion by the rules and regulations. Twelve stated that they were simply uninterested or were just "planning to die"; they saw no use in voting. Another five cited the lack of transportation or poor health as reasons for not registering to vote. The remaining six respondents cited other reasons. Thus, most attributed their lack of voter registration to procedural factors (citizenship or illiteracy) rather than apathy or functional disability (immobility). More respondents voted in national elections than in local or state elections.[11] Among the respondents who voted in past elections, 23 voted regularly in national elections, 16 in state elections, and 15 in local elections. Compared to the general white population 65 and over and an Hispanic sample from Los Angeles (all age groups), the San Jose sample rates low on voting frequency (Table 15).

83

TABLE 15

VOTING RATES OF WHITE AGED, LOS ANGELES HISPANICS,
AND THE SAN JOSE SAMPLE
(Percentage)

	Los Angeles Hispanics[a] (All Age Groups)	White Aged[b] (Over 65)	San Jose[c] Sample
Percentage voting in national elections	49.9	68	37

a) Grebler et al. (1970:564).

b) Data from a Survey Research Center survey, cited in Campbell (1971:113).

c) Thirty-seven percent represents 23 respondents who voted regularly in national elections out of 63 respondents who stated their voting frequency in past national elections.

Past political activities

As part of developing a profile on political behavior, Milbrath's "Hierarchy of Political Involvement" was used to measure past political activities. Milbrath (1965) divides his hierarchy into three sections: gladiatorial, transitional, and spectator. The activities in the gladiatorial category represent the most active activities in which an individual may engage, the spectator category represents the least active activities, and the transitional category includes activities which could be either gladiatorial or spectator, depending on the situation. These three categories are mutually exclusive--that is, if a person says he has gone to a political meeting he is given a mark in only one of the

84

three categories. The hierarchy is further subdivided
into three categories of political orientation:
Hispanic, old age, and general citizenship.

For the transitional activities and most of the
gladiatorial activities, except for "candidate" and
"held office," the activities centered on Hispanic
related politics. Only in old-age related politics had
anyone held office or been a candidate; the positions
were with the city and state aging commissions. In the
spectator categories, by a large margin, past political
activities had centered on general citizenship politics
with Hispanic politics placing second.

In general, 20 respondents had participated in
various gladiatorial activities, mostly participation
in Hispanic related politics; 23 in various
transitional activities; and 52 in various spectator
activities, mostly general citizenship. These figures
show types of activity most engaged in and the
particular orientation of that activity over an
unspecified time period. Thus, making comparisons with
other groups is difficult.

Understanding the political climate of the
respondents' youth might elucidate their emphasis on
Hispanic politics. During the first half of this
century, politics in the Southwest was characterized by
discrimination, intimidation, and electoral barriers.
Usually, general citizenship or "establishment"
politics excluded Hispanic participation. Interviews
revealed that some, at one time or another, had engaged
in "protest" activities such as voter registration
drives, union organizing, and protest marches. The
data from the hierarchy substantiate this: nine and 16
respondents, respectively, had participated in
demonstrations and rallies related to Hispanic
politics. Protest activities were especially
characteristic of those from New Mexico and
Texas.[12]

This suggests that some of today's Hispanic aged,
at least in this sample, although considered by some
Hispanics as unsympathetic to the Hispanic movement and
Hispanic politics, actually have employed similar forms
of political action to those used by contemporary
Hispanics (strikes, protests, etc.). This also
suggests that although general citizenship politics
(transitional and gladiatorial) and old-age politics
may be alien to the elderly, Hispanic politics

(transitional and gladiatorial) are not. Thus, some older Hispanics have a tradition of interest in Hispanic related politics and may manifest it in support for contemporary Hispanic issues, assuming they are not discouraged.

Social participation in church and senior activities

Participation in the church and church organizations was much higher than in civic groups, political groups, or unions. Fifty-one percent attend church regularly, and 29 percent attend infrequently.[13] Seven percent reported active membership in the Cursillistas and 6 percent reported active membership in the Guadalupanas, two major Hispanic church groups which act as social-religious organizations in the San Jose area.

Three senior citizen groups in San Jose are predominantly Hispanic. The Libertad Club is located on the East side; the other two, Gardner Center and Alma Center, are both located in the West side. Only nine respondents were active members of these three senior groups: five in the Libertad Club and two each in the Alma and Gardner Centers.

Index of political activity

Indices are useful measures of aggregate responses when no single indicator is likely to be capable of capturing the central meaning intended. They are developed by collapsing variables according to a particular concept in use (in this case political participation), assigning a weight to each variable, and adding up the scores. In this section indices for each of the various political activities provide a composite score for each respondent's level of political participation and facilitate the task of measuring relationships between the dependent and independent variables. These indices measure the respondent's level of political activity on a scale of low, medium, or high. The three categories are created by assigning weights to the variables within each dimension of political participation, adding the scores, and dividing by three. Table 16 provides breakdowns on familiarity with and support of leaders and organizations, discussion of politics, total vote frequency, and extent of participation in past political activities (Hispanic politics, old-age politics, general citizenship). In addition,

TABLE 16

INDEX OF POLITICAL ACTIVITY

	Number	Low		Medium		High	
		N	%	N	%	N	%
Familiarity	106	60	56	38	37	8	7
Support	81	48	59	30	37	3	4
Talk politics	105	71	67	21	20	13	13
Total vote frequency	63	36	57	12	19	15	24
Hispanic political activities	98	83	85	9	9	6	6
Old-age political activities	94	89	95	2	2	3	3
General citizen political activities	99	87	88	9	9	3	3

87

membership in church groups and senior citizen clubs
are indexed on a yes/no dichotomy (see Table 17).

TABLE 17

INDEX OF OTHER ACTIVITY

Membership	Number	Yes		No	
		N	%	N	%
Church group	104	26	25	78	75
Senior club	104	14	13	90	87

The indices reveal that the respondents rated most
active in voting and discussion of politics. Fifteen
respondents and 13 respondents rated high in voting and
discussion of politics, respectively. Six respondents
also rated high in Hispanic political activities,
versus three for old-age politics.

Summary

The data reveal that the sample is generally
inactive in political participation when compared to
other groups, but that on certain dimensions the
respondents are fairly active. For example, political
awareness is higher than expected. The sample is most
familiar with the Libertad Club and the UFW and their
leaders, Chavez and Sarinana, and least familiar with
MAPA, La Confederacion, Corky Gonzalez, and Angel
Gutierrez, the more militant organizations and
leaders. The greatest support was for the Libertad
Center and the UFW and their leaders, Chavez and
Sarinana, with the least support for La Raza Unida
Party, La Confederacion, Gutierrez, and Gonzalez. This
section has suggested that familiarity and support are
based more on the relevance these groups have to older
persons than on ideology. When compared to that of the
White elderly and Hispanics in general, political
interest rated favorably. Membership in political
groups also rated favorably for this sample as compared
to White elderly and Hispanics in general, but the San

Jose group was low on civic group membership. Voting frequency was found to rate low when compared to the voting of White aged and Los Angeles Hispanics. In addition, this sample's past political activities have centered on Hispanic related politics, and more older persons have engaged in spectator activities than in transitional or gladiatorial activities. In terms of social participation, few of these older Hispanics are members of a senior club, but a total of 13 percent are members of the two major Hispanic church groups in San Jose.

Part III: Political Attitudes

This part explores political attitudes of the Hispanic elderly for two purposes: (1) to discover the sample's feelings about the current political situation of Hispanics in general and the Hispanic aged, and (2) to explain political participation or lack of participation by the Hispanic aged. Their attitudes allow for exploring the predispositions aged Hispanics have toward various forms of political activities, ideologies, and the political behavior of other groups. Attitudinal questions asked in this study focus on three key areas: Hispanic politics and generational relations, senior citizen affairs, and the status position of the Hispanics aged.[14]

Hispanic politics and generational relations

This study anticipates that the elderly do not participate in Hispanic politics because they feel alienated from the political ideology of younger Hispanics; thus, the study explores the attitudes of elderly Hispanics toward the Hispanic movement, its politics, and their feelings about generational conflicts.

To determine the degree of attitudinal support for various forms of Hispanic political activities, three questions were asked. They focused on organizing for achievement of rights, electing Hispanics to public office, and active demonstrations and confrontations to voice inequities against Hispanics. Eighty-three percent of those who answered these questions agreed Hispanics should organize, while only 46 percent agreed Hispanics need to actively demonstrate (see Table 18). This suggests that the older person may fear violence and militant action, feelings characteristic of a politics of deference.

TABLE 18

DEGREE OF ATTITUDINAL SUPPORT FOR HISPANIC POLITICS

Attitude	Number	Yes		No	
		N	%	N	%
1. Agree Hispanics should organize?	60	50	83	10	17
2. Agree Hispanics should be elected?	60	51	85	9	15
3. Agree Hispanics should protest?	56	26	46	30	54

An index was created from these three categories to determine whether the respondents were high, medium, or low in terms of attitudinal support.[15]   Table 19 indicates that a higher number of respondents rated high than rated medium or low.

Table 19

INDEX OF DEGREE OF ATTITUDINAL SUPPORT FOR HISPANIC POLITICS
(N=67)

Degree of Support	Number	Percentage
Low	20	30
Medium	21	31
High	26	39

The sample was asked to comment on why few

Hispanic older persons were actively involved in Hispanic politics (see Table 20). Contrary to the assumption that older Hispanics would not participate because of fear, ideological disagreements, or generational conflicts, the highest number of responses (25), among the 67 who responded, cited a lack of communication (see total frequency). For example, the older person feels uninformed about current issues, he does not understand what the Hispanic movement is, or he feels that no one has made an effort to contact him. The next highest number of responses (see total frequency) dealt with fear (21) and negative role expectations (18). For example, the older person is afraid that if he does get involved he will lose his Social Security or be deported or he feels that it is not his role to be involved because he should be involved only with the family or the church. Ideological disagreements (12) and generational conflicts (13) received a lower number of responses than fear and lack of communication. Lowest of all the categories were those dealing with poor self-image--the feeling that one is too old or that if one does get involved, no one else would care.

Since the study hypothesized that generational conflicts are an important factor in the noninvolvement of the elderly in Hispanic politics, a number of items were developed to shed light on this issue. The items included the importance to the elderly of the political issues supported by Hispanic activists and the understanding of the old by the young. To the former item, of 61 who responded, 23 (38 percent) agreed that the political issues were relevant to them; the majority felt otherwise. Of the 27 who elaborated on their responses (both negative and positive), 10 felt that Hispanic activists and leaders, by striving for their goals, were helping all Hispanics, including the older persons. Two felt that Hispanic leaders were doing good things, but should not resort to violence. Of those who did not feel that Hispanics were dealing with relevant issues, six felt that Hispanics care about no one else, least of all the older person. Another nine felt that the Hispanics were not really effective and were too disorganized to help anyone. To the second item, of the 81 who responded, 59 (73 percent) agreed that younger Hispanics did not understand their elders. Their explanation for the lack of understanding was that Hispanics were becoming assimilated, and thus were losing their respect for older persons and making no effort to communicate with

91

TABLE 20

WHY IS THE OLDER HISPANIC NOT IN THE
HISPANIC MOVEMENT?

(N=67)

Reason	Reason I		Reason II		Total Frequency
	N	%	N	%	
Negative role expectations	14	21	4	13	18
Communication	19	28	6	19	25
Ideology	11	16	1	3	12
Generational	9	13	4	13	13
Fear	9	13	12	39	21
Poor self-image	4	6	4	13	8
Other	1	1	0	0	1
Total		98		100	98

the elderly. Moreover, the respondents often believed that youth were different because their values were more congruent with this country's; thus, assimilation caused differences and loss of the traditional culture even though youth were still basically good.

Senior citizen affairs

An assumption of this study is that the older Hispanic has not developed an age-group consciousness because of traditional ties to the extended family and that because of this, participation in senior centers and age related politics is minimal. This section assesses the attitudes of the older person toward involvement in senior activities and toward participating in age related politics.

To determine the respondents' degree of attitudinal support for age related politics, three questions were put to them. These questions focused on whether they would support efforts by Hispanic senior clubs to lobby in the state legislature, to donate money to the UFW, and to encourage members to picket for the UFW. Table 21 shows that 66 percent of those who responded would support the trip to the legislature, while 46 percent would support picketing. The respondents, however, tended to have a strong allegiance to the farm worker movement because of their previous occupation and their location in San Jose; thus, the two questions referring to the UFW reflected a skewed response.

In addition, 36 respondents explained why they felt as they did. Among those (15) who would support all or most of these activities, eight cited the need for older persons to organize and be involved in politics and seven cited the need to support the UFW. Twelve of the 21 respondents who would not support these activities felt either that it was inappropriate for older Hispanics to be politically active, or that since the family takes care of its elderly, politics is unnecessary, or that God "is the answer" to whatever problems need resolution (negative role expectations). The remaining nine felt that older persons could be hurt or exploited if they became involved.

TABLE 21

DEGREE OF ATTITUDINAL SUPPORT FOR
SENIOR ACTIVITIES

Attitude	Number	Yes		No	
		N	%	N	%
1. Support of lobbying	56	37	66	19	34
2. Support of donation to UFW	51	31	61	20	39
3. Support of picketing	54	25	46	29	54

The three questions provide a picture of
attitudinal support for participation of Hispanic
elderly in political activities. A composite picture
of this attitudinal support was obtained by creating an
index which listed each respondent as low, medium, or
high, according to how he responded on the three
questions.[16] Table 22 shows that of the 57
respondents, 24 (42 percent) rated high, as compared
with 26 (46 percent) who rated low. Again, the strong
support for Chavez may have inflated the high scores.

TABLE 22

INDEX OF DEGREE OF ATTITUDINAL SUPPORT
FOR SENIOR ACTIVITIES
(N=57)

Degree of Support	Number	Percentage
Low	26	46
Medium	7	12
High	24	42

Two projective questions were asked to determine how the respondents felt about older Hispanics participating in senior groups, about their participating with Whites, and about the degree to which they might become involved in senior political activities. The first projective statement read: "There is a Mexican-American senior citizen club on the East side. They are trying to bring together older people so that they can get to know each other. Do you agree that they should?" Of 81 who responded to this question, 65 (80 percent) agreed and 16 (20 percent) disagreed. They were then asked to explain why they felt as they did. Thirty-seven respondents provided an explanation. Most (20) agreed that the Hispanic aged should participate to have recreation, to help each other, and to meet friends (social activities), and eight felt the older Hispanic should become involved in community activities. Of those that disagreed, the responses were almost evenly divided between negative role expectations (five) and poor self-image (four). For example, some felt that the Hispanic aged should not participate because the family takes care of the older person and it is not appropriate for older persons to be involved with politics and organizations. Others felt they could not participate because they were too old and useless or because it would not benefit them. Six respondents also provided a second reason. Of those offering second explanations, two mentioned the need for social activities, three mentioned the need to participate in community and political activities, and one felt the older person did not need to be involved because the family takes care of the elderly.

A second question was: "If Whites were involved in this group would you still join?" Of 56 who answered, 21 (38 percent) stated they would; they explained that the Hispanic aged should not segregate themselves since all people are the same. However, 35 (63 percent) stated they would not; they explained that Whites are racist and not to be trusted or that even though Whites may not be racist, cultural differences would make it impractical for Whites and Hispanics to be together.

To discover from the respondents why more Hispanic elderly were not involved in senior citizen clubs, a statement about the Hispanic aged not participating in senior citizen activities was presented to them and they were asked to comment on it. The large number

95

(82) responding to this question presented a variety of
views which may help dispel some myths about why some
Hispanic aged do not participate in senior citizen
activities.

Table 23 presents the responses in seven
categories. Since many gave two reasons, both are
provided and added. The highest frequency of responses
(25) was given by those who feel the Hispanic aged do
not get involved because they consider themselves old,
feel that no one cares about their contribution, or are
apathetic (poor self-image and apathy). The next
highest frequency of responses (23) related to poor
communication and illiteracy. Those who cited these
reasons feel the older person lacks information, needs
to be organized, or is illiterate (or does not speak
English). Another large number of responses were given
by those who cited negative role expectations (21) and
functional capabilities (17). They feel the older
person considers the home and church most important or
he lacks transportation and is in poor health. The
fewest responses occurred among those who feel the aged
Hispanic are distrustful (eight) or afraid (13) to be
involved.

Status position of the Hispanic aged

A third area of attitudinal exploration concerned
the problems the older Hispanic perceive they have and
the strategies they feel will effectively confront
these problems. Table 24 presents those problems most
frequently suggested. The sample tended to believe
that old age exacerbated these problems.

The first reason most frequently cited as a
problem of the aged is health. Two other problems most
frequently mentioned, money and mobility, are clearly
linked to health problems. Lack of money often
prohibits good health practices, while poor health may
prohibit great mobility. Moreover, these three
problems form a web of interrelationships, each
affecting the other.

Concerning the total frequency responses, mobility
and money continue to be the most important problems of
the aged. Since lack of income inhibits access to all
other resources and since this group experiences
unusually low income status, these responses are not
surprising. The income problem enlarges the mobility
problem since low income limits car ownership; limited

TABLE 23

WHY DO HISPANIC AGED NOT PARTICIPATE
IN SENIOR ACTIVITIES?
(N=82)

Reason	Reason I		Reason II		Total Frequency
	N	%	N	%	
Functional	13	16	4	15	17
Communication (illiteracy)	16	20	7	27	23
Poor image and apathy	19	23	6	23	25
Negative role expectations	16	20	5	19	21
Fear	9	11	4	15	13
Distrust	8	10	0	0	8
Other	1	1	0	0	1
Total	101		99		108

TABLE 24

WHAT PROBLEMS DO HISPANIC AGED HAVE?
(N=61)

Problem	Reason I		Reason II		Total Frequency
	N	%	N	%	
Housing	3	5	4	11	7
Mobility	13	21	13	34	26
Health	19	31	0	0	19
Money	13	21	13	34	26
Loneliness	3	5	5	13	8
Need for social services	2	3	0	0	2
Other	8	13	3	8	11
Total		99		100	99

mobility is further exacerbated by the poor intraurban transportation system of San Jose.

Concerning these problems, the sample was asked to suggest possible strategies for their alleviation. Fifty-six respondents suggested possible approaches. Table 25 shows the categories of responses. Because the answers were framed in terms of both societal responsibility to the problem and individual responsibility, the question was ambiguous. Thus, the responses ranged from the responsibility of traditional support systems (family, church) and governmental support systems (social services, educational institutions) to political action in which the older person would become involved in political activities or advocacy. However, because the question did measure the types of responsibilities the respondents would take in proposing strategies for resolving problems faced by the elderly Hispanic, the question was maintained.

In Table 25 the total frequency column shows that political action received 20 responses and advocacy 17. Familial received 10, and social services and education combined received 20 responses. Underscoring the significance of this question, Chapter IV will reveal that those who mentioned the need for political action or advocacy were most likely to be politically active and that those who mentioned the need for "familial" support were more likely to be politically inactive.

To obtain data on the potential of these respondents to become active and to accept the idea that other elderly Hispanics should become more active, two questions which related to these issues were asked. First, did they feel that older persons needed special groups and organizations to look out for their needs and rights? Of 65 who responded, 54 (83 percent) said "Yes," and 11 (17 percent) said "No." The second question asked: "Would you join an organization designed to do more for older persons?" A large number, 70, answered this question; 33 (47 percent) said they would, and 37 (53 percent) said they would not.

Summary

This section revealed that attitudinal support for Hispanic politics existed, although most respondents felt older Hispanics were not currently involved in

TABLE 25

HOW SHOULD PROBLEMS FACED BY AGED HISPANICS
BE RESOLVED?
(N=56)

Response	Reason I		Reason II		Total Frequency
	N	%	N	%	
Political action	19	34	1	6	20
Advocacy	9	16	8	50	17
Familial	9	16	1	6	10
Social services	10	18	2	13	12
Education	6	11	2	13	8
Senior centers	3	5	1	6	4
Other	0	0	1	6	1
Total	100		100		72

100

Hispanic related politics because of a lack of communication and fear of negative consequences (46 of total responses in Table 20). In addition, 38 respondents felt that Hispanics were not dealing with issues important to them, and 59 respondents felt that younger Hispanics did not understand the older person.

Support existed for involvement by elderly Hispanics in age related activities. Twenty respondents agreed that older Hispanics should organize around social activities. Less sympathy, however, was given to the idea of working with the White elderly. Thirty-five respondents felt that cultural differences and racism negated cooperation between White and Hispanic elderly.

Respondents perceived their major problems as the lack of money and inadequate transportation (52 of total responses in Table 24). Most of the respondents who stated strategies to meet these problems placed the responsibility on governmental (social services, educational services) or traditional support systems (family) (30 of total responses in Table 25) rather than on political actions (20 of total responses in Table 25). However, a number of respondents, when asked if older Hispanics need special groups and would they join them, answered in the affirmative (54 and 33, respectively).

Summary and Interpretation

Contrary to the review of literature and the researcher's personal experiences, actual political participation, political awareness, and political interest of the Hispanic elderly is higher than expected. In comparison with White aged and samples from the general Hispanic population, the Hispanic aged from San Jose are relatively inactive in terms of membership in formal organizations (civic and political groups and unions) and voting, although their degree of political awareness (familiarity and support) and political interest (discussion of politics) compares favorably. Therefore, the hypothesis, that because of their social, economic, cultural, and political position, the elderly Hispanic will be found to cluster near the low end of the hierarchy of political involvement, is supported—with the following qualifications: the Hispanic aged are relatively inactive in actual political participation but rate favorably on political awareness and political

101

interest. In part, the high degree of political awareness exhibited by the sample may spring from the long history of political activism in the barrios of San Jose (See Appendix A for description of political activism in San Jose). In examining the political awareness and political participation of this sample, one must note that San Jose presents a unique political climate. Yet a portion of the sample clearly did not first acquire a political awareness in San Jose, but had been involved in various political actions when they were younger. For example, 20 to 23 of the sample had participated in gladiatorial and transitional activities.

Data revealed support for Hispanic political action: 47 respondents rated medium or high on the index of attitudinal support for Hispanic politics. Many older Hispanics in the sample supported efforts by Hispanics to organize and effect political change. This support was indicated by the political awareness of the sample. Close to half (50) of the sample was familiar with some of the Hispanic leaders and organizations mentioned, while up to 55 respondents supported at least two of these leaders and organizations. These findings complement those found in the exploration of past political behavior. That exploration discovered that in past political activities older Hispanics had concentrated on Hispanic related politics. These findings imply that this sample has maintained a continuity of political interest and support for Hispanic politics into old age. In other words, Hispanics who had actively supported past Hispanic political issues tended to support contemporary Hispanic political issues. This is substantiated by examining the relation between those who rated medium and high on an index of attitudinal support for Hispanic politics and those who rated medium and high on an index measuring participation in past Hispanic politics.[17]
Findings revealed that five of six who rated high in past Hispanic political activities also rated high on attitudinal support. Among the six who rated medium in past Hispanic political activities, five rated high on attitudinal support. Thus, within this sample, those who support today's Hispanic were also active in past Hispanic related politics.

Some significant findings in the exploration of the respondents' attitudes toward Hispanic politics appeared in reasons stated for alleged noninvolvement by elderly in Hispanic politics. Contrary to this study's assumption that the Hispanic aged would be reluctant to participate because of ideological disagreements and generational conflicts, the responses cited lack of communication and fear as the major reasons. Thus two hypotheses -- that because of discouragement (generational conflicts) by younger Hispanics, the level of participation in Hispanic politics for older Hispanics will be low; and that because of ideological disagreement with the "Hispanic Political Movement," older Hispanics will express negative attitudes toward Hispanics politics -- are refuted.

Attitudinal support for participation by the Hispanic elderly in senior activities is also present, as shown by 31 respondents who rated medium or high on this index. Actual participation in senior citizen groups, however, was only 2 to 5 percent of the sample. The contradiction between attitudinal support and participation in senior centers is probably related to two factors: long-term organizing of senior centers in the barrios of San Jose and a continued traditional reliance on the family and church. For social and emotional support, the Hispanic elderly have not traditionally relied on age-segregated groups. Instead, they have been integral parts of the social and political life of the community and family. Thus, any participation by the elderly in senior centers would tend to be low. Nevertheless, for the last eight years various persons in San Jose have worked hard to encourage older Hispanics to form senior centers based on their common needs. The high attitudinal support expressed by the sample indicates the effects of this organizing. Actual involvement in senior centers is still difficult to achieve. Ramona Sarinana, director of a Hispanic senior center, attests that getting the older Hispanic involved is difficult. It has taken her eight years to build the Libertad Club to a membership of approximately 500 older Hispanics. She realized that senior centers were alien to the older person. That apathy, poor self-image, and negative role expectations were the most frequent reasons cited for the noninvolvement of older persons shows further the alienation older Hispanics continue to feel about senior centers and senior activities.

Footnotes -- Chapter III

1. A substantial percentage (14 percent)--conspicuous by their lucidity, articulateness, and cooperativeness as compared to the total sample -- were between 81 and 88 years old. The respondents over 65, for the most part, provide the richest accounts of personal political experiences.

2. The Handbook of Labor Statistics from the Department of Labor, 1975, utilized $2,590 as the poverty level of one person.

3. Unless otherwise stated, percentages are based on an N for the total sample (N=106).

4. Before 1960 the Santa Clara Valley was primarily agricultural. Many Hispanic migrants came to this valley to work the crops. However, the valley rapidly became urbanized to the point where only a small percentage of the agricultural land remained. Those migrants who did not leave the area either turned to the fruit and vegetable canneries or to unskilled urban occupations for employment.

5. The 1980 Census found that 81 percent of persons of Spanish origin reside in metropolitan areas.

6. U.S. Department of Commerce, Bureau of the Census, Current Population Report (1970) (Washington, D.C.: Government Printing Office, October, 1971).

7. Taken from a special report, "Mexican-American," Business Week, May 29, 1971.

8. The Aging Population of Santa Clara County: A Study. (San Jose: Social Planning Council of Santa Clara County, Inc., 1973), p.17.

9. The numbers in parentheses refer to those who stated they were familiar with the particular individual or organization. See Appendix C for complete tables of familiarity and support of the leaders and organizations.

10. See Appendix C for table on membership in formal organizations.

11. See Appendix C for table on voting frequencies.

12. See Appendix C for rates of political activities on the hierarchy of political involvement.

13. See Appendix C for tables on church activities.

14. See Appendix D for definitions of attitudinal categories used in this section.

15. The three items (categories) in the index were assigned a weighted score according to the perceived likelihood of the older person agreeing to a particular activity. Thus, item 3 was weighted most heavily because it was thought the respondent would be least likely to agree; item 2 next, and item 1 least heavily because it was felt the respondent would be most likely to agree. The weights were then summed and divided by three.

16. The three items in this index were weighted in the same manner as the items in the index on attitudinal support for Hispanic politics. These weights were then summed and divided by three. The index in Table 22 assigned the highest weight to item 3 because it was thought the respondent was least likely to agree with picketing, the next weight to item 2, and the least weight to item 1, because it was felt the respondent would be more receptive to lobbying.

17. Before the development of an index measuring overall past political activities, separate indices were developed for each of the three variables (general citizenship, old age, Hispanic related) comprising the index of past political participation.

CHAPTER IV

ANALYSIS OF CHARACTERISTICS OF THE POLITICALLY ACTIVE AND POLITICALLY INACTIVE

This chapter will examine specific characteristics of the politically active and politically inactive respondents. Chapter III showed the Hispanic elderly to be relatively inactive on some indices and fairly active on others. For example, eight rated high on familiarity, three rated high on support, 15 rated high on voting, three rated high on past political activities related to old age and general citizenship politics, six rated high on past political activities related to Hispanic politics, and 13 rated high on discussion of politics and public problems. In addition, a few respondents were active members of civic and political groups and senior citizen clubs. Who are the active respondents, and how do they differ from the nonactive ones? What are their characteristics, and what can these characteristics reveal about the political behavior of older Hispanics?

The review of the literature revealed various factors which may account for variation in political participation among older Hispanics. These include factors affecting a sense of involvement in the political system such as ethnic identification and political acculturation, factors affecting a sense of involvement in Hispanic politics such as generational conflicts, and factors affecting access to participation such as socioeconomic status. In addition, a person's sense of political efficacy was also identified as necessary for him to be motivated enough to participate. To determine which of these independent variables are more closely related to the active and to the inactive respondents, this chapter will explore the relationships of the independent variables to the dependent variable of political participation. First, the chapter will examine socioeconomic status, ethnic identification, geographical location, and political efficacy. Then it will deal with attitudinal characteristics.

In the previous chapter indices were constructed

107

for specific dependent variables. This chapter
utilizes two new indices which clump together the
various dependent variables into two overall indices:
current political participation and past political
participation. These two indices were constructed to
rate each respondent, depending on his level of
political activity, as nonactive or active, in both
past and current political participation. Table 26
shows the respondents' ratings on these indices.
Throughout the analysis the indices of current and past
political participation will be used in measuring the
relationships between political participation and the
independent variables.

TABLE 26

INDEX OF CURRENT AND PAST POLITICAL PARTICIPATION

	Current Political Participation[a]		Past Political Participation[b]	
	N	%	N	%
Nonactive	81	76	80	80
Active	25	24	20	20
Total	106		100	

[a]Includes dimensions of membership in formal
organizations, voting, awareness, and discussion of
politics.

[b]Includes dimensions of past political activities:
Hispanic related politics, old-age related politics,
and general citizenship.

Part I: Profiles of the Politically
Active and Inactive

Socioeconomic status

The sex of a respondent did not differentiate
political participation either in the past or in the
present. The actives (p > .5) were almost equally
divided between men (13) and women (12) on the index of
current political participation. On the index of past
political participation, eight women and 12 men rated

108

active (p < .210).

Respondents 50 to 65 years old were significantly more active on current political participation than those 66 years and over (X^2 = 16.225, p < .013). Sixteen (64 percent) of the 25 actives were between 50 and 65 years. One explanation for the greater number of actives 50-65 years is that they are physically more able to travel and can maintain better health than those over 65 years. Political activism was not, however, exclusively the domain of the younger segment of the sample. A number of those over 65 were also politically interested and aware (36 percent of the actives). For example, 14 of those registered to vote (N = 39), and five who rated high on voting frequency (N = 15) were 66 and over. On the variables of familiarity, support, and discussion of politics, those 66 and over were well represented. Three who scored high on familiarity (N = 8), two of the three who rated high on support, and five of 13 who rated high on political discussions were also over 66. Thus, even though those under 66 were physically more active, those over 65 continue to be politically aware in terms of familiarity, support, discussion of politics, and voting.

Education was a statistically significant factor in the current political participation of the sample. Of those with no education, 22 (28 percent) were nonactives; four (16 percent) were actives. Of those with 1-12 years of education, 56 (72 percent) were nonactives; 20 (80 percent) were actives (X^2 = 8.205, p < .043).

The respondents were categorized in four past occupations characteristic of the sample: farmworker, housewife, sheds (canneries, packing houses), and urban occupations (janitors, unskilled labor). Those with these various occupations showed no significant difference (p < .134). Seventy-nine percent of the actives and 91 percent of the nonactives were not working.

Those with higher incomes were significantly more likely to be active than those with lower incomes. Table 27 shows that 19 (80 percent) of the actives were receiving at least $4,000 versus 24 of the nonactives (32 percent) who were receiving at least $4,000.

TABLE 27

INCOME OF RESPONDENTS
(N=98)

| Income | Current Political Participation | | | |
| | Nonactive (N=74) | | Actives (N=24) | |
	N	%	N	%
$1,000-1,999	3	4	1	4
$2,000-2,999	32	43	3	13
$3,000-3,999	15	20	1	4
$4,000-4,999	12	16	4	17
$5,000-5,999	4	5	4	17
$6,000-6,999	8	11	7	29
$7,000-10,000	0	0	4	17

x^2 = 26.815, p < .001.

Ethnic identification

Ethnic identification should determine whether the nonactives are more closely identified with Mexico than the actives, as well as determine which variables are more significantly related to political participation. Ethnic identification is composed of the following variables: birthplace, recentness of immigration and frequency of visits to Mexico.

The data showed a significant relationship between birthplace and degree of political participation. Table 28 shows that those born in the United States were more likely to be active currently than those born in Mexico. An examination of the country the respondents were raised in underscores this finding. Those raised in the United States were more likely to be active than those raised in Mexico.

Time of arrival in the United States was not significantly related to current political participation. At no specific period did the politically active first arrive, nor at any specific period did the politically inactive arrive. Among a total of seven actives, four came between 1911-1920 and three came between 1921-1950.

The data showed no significant relationship between the frequency Mexico is visited and the degree of political participation. Among the actives, 60 percent never or rarely visit; and among the inactives, 68 percent rarely or never visit.

TABLE 28

COUNTRY RESPONDENTS WERE BORN AND RAISED IN

| Current Political Participation | Country Born in (N=106)[a] | | | |
| | United States | | Mexico | |
	N	%	N	%
Nonactive (N=81)	27	33	54	67
Active (N=25)	18	72	7	28

| | Country Raised in (N=105)[b] | | | |
| | United States | | Mexico | |
	N	%	N	%
Nonactive (N=80)	26	33	54	68
Active (N=25)	16	64	9	36

[a]X^2 = 11.691, p < .001.

[b]X^2 = 7.875, p < .006.

Geographical Location

In addition to findings that age, income, education, and birthplace are significantly related to political participation, it was also found that geographical location (residential location and the particular state raised in) played a part in the political behavior of the sample.

The literature shows that those raised in urban areas are more likely to be politically active than those raised in rural areas (Milbrath, 1965). This sample showed a significant difference between those raised in rural areas and those raised in urban areas (X^2 = 4.104, p < .043). Of those politically active, 63 percent were raised in urban areas; 39 percent of the nonactives were raised in urban areas. More important, the neighborhood a respondent lives in and the state he came from directly relates to the degree of political participation.

The random selection of the sample population chose respondents from three different parts of the city: the East side, the West side, and the Park area.[1] The East and West sides comprise the two major barrios of San Jose; a high degree of political activity and senior organizing exist in these two areas. In contrast, the Park area is more conservative. This area, a mixture of White and Hispanic families, has few political and senior activities. Respondents from the politically active East and West sides were more active than those from the politically inactive Park area. Table 29 shows that 96 percent of the actives lived in the East and West sides, while only 4 percent lived in the Park area. On the other hand, 24 percent of the nonactives lived in the Park area.

TABLE 29

SAN JOSE NEIGHBORHOOD (BARRIO) RESIDED
IN BY RESPONDENTS
(N=100)

Current Political Participation	West Side		Park Area		East Side	
	N	%	N	%	N	%
Nonactive (N=76)	29	38	18	24	29	38
Active (N=24)	11	46	1	4	12	50

The data suggest that the neighborhood where one lives has some influence on an older person's political behavior. Various writers (Litwak & Szeleny, 1968;

Gans, 1962; Shuttles, 1968) have alluded to the neighborhood's effect on human behavior. They see the neighborhood and its activities as influencing the behavior of its residents. In addition to the possible influence of the neighborhood on political behavior, Galarza et al. (1970) mention that the barrio also serves a mutual help purpose. He points out that in the barrios mutual help is the pattern and that this has always been immediate, concrete, and practical. He cites as an example the establishment and the maintenance of cooperative child care arrangements in which the grandparents have an important function. Through her study of grandparents in the barrios of Denver, Sotomayor (1973) also found that mutual help was the important aspect of the neighborhood for the older person.

If a neighborhood is defined as a "small community characterized by limited area and highly developed face to face relations" (Fairchild, 1944), then the East and West sides can be termed cohesive neighborhoods. The political history of the East and West sides attests to a sense of community. Thus, the findings above suggest that if the older Hispanic lives in a politically active and cohesive barrio (neighborhood) and identifies with it, he will be more likely to participate politically than one who does not live in such a neighborhood. Of course, a different conclusion is possible; the actives might have chosen the East and West sides precisely because of these areas' political activity. Either way, the influence of the neighborhood remains, and the suggestions of a positive relationship between neighborhood and political behavior remains plausible.

When related to political participation, state birthplace was an important variable. New Mexico-born respondents were the most active. The frequency with which those from New Mexico rated high on most dimensions of political and social participation shows them to be the most active respondents. Table 30 shows that on almost every dimension of political and social participation New Mexicans formed a substantial proportion of those who were members of organizations or who rated high on a political dimension.

New Mexicans' high political activity may be traceable to the political climate in that state; since its founding, New Mexico has maintained its Spanish/New Mexican heritage and has continued to maintain

TABLE 30
POLITICAL ACTIVISM BY NEW MEXICANS

Dimensions of Political Participation	New Mexicans		
	Total Number	N	%
Membership in unions	2	1	50
Membership in political groups	6	4	66
Membership in civic groups	4	2	50
Voting (high rating)	13	4	31
Familiarity (high rating)	6	3	50
Discussion of politics (high rating)	8	5	63
Past political activities:			
Chicano-related (high rating)	4	2	50
Old-age-related (high rating)	2	2	100
General citizenship (high rating)	1	1	100
Dimension of Social Participation			
Membership in senior clubs (high rating)	7	3	43
Index of Current Political Participation	10	4	40
Index of Past Political Participation	18	6	33

extensive participation by its Hispanic population in local and state politics.² Among the states in the Southwest, it is the most politicized in terms of Hispanic related polities. New Mexicans' political environment allows opportunities for involvement in politics. Thus, the political socialization resulting from exposure to these political stimuli probably encourages the political participation of the elderly who have left the state and now live in San Jose.

Political efficacy and citizen duty

A sense of political efficacy and a sense of citizen duty are the feelings that one's actions can make a difference and that one has an obligation to participate. They are directly related to political participation: those with higher levels are more likely to be active. Therefore, Chapter II hypothesized that the politically active respondent would have a higher sense of political efficacy and citizen duty than the nonactive. The data bear this out. The politically active were found to have a significantly greater sense of political efficacy and sense of citizen duty than the nonactive. Table 31 shows that 58 percent of the actives received a political efficacy score of three or higher versus 9 percent for the nonactives.³ In addition, 50 percent of the actives versus 11 percent of the nonactives received a score of three or higher on the scale of citizen duty.

These findings indicate that among the sample of Hispanic aged a sense of efficacy and citizen duty is important to participation.

Summary

The analysis of the relationships between specific independent variables--socioeconomic status, ethnic identification, geographic location, political efficacy--and the dependent variable of political participation reveals that particular variables are significantly related to the actives and to the nonactives.

In the political science literature, several socioeconomic correlates were identified as relating significantly to political participation. These correlates were tested against an index of current participation and past participation. Among the

TABLE 31

POLITICAL EFFICACY AND CITIZEN DUTY

Current Political Participation	Political Efficacy Scores[a] (N=66)											
	0		1		2		3		4		5	
	N	%	N	%	N	%	N	%	N	%	N	%
Nonactive (N=45)	14	31	13	29	14	31	3	7	1	2	0	0
Active (N=21)	3	14	5	24	1	5	4	19	6	29	2	10

	Citizen Duty Scores[b] (N=54)									
	0		1		2		3		4	
	N	%	N	%	N	%	N	%	N	%
Nonactive (N=36)	7	19	13	36	12	33	1	3	3	8
Active (N=18)	1	6	3	17	5	28	7	39	2	11

$aX^2 = 21.811$, p $<$ .001.

$bX^2 = 13.874$, p $<$ .008.

116

correlates--sex, income, education, occupation, age--only education, income, and age were significantly related. Respondents who earned $4,000 and more, had a high school education, and were 50-65 years old were the most likely to be politically active. Concerning the age correlate, a substantial number of those over 65 were fairly active on both the index of current political participation and several dimensions of political activities such as voting and awareness. That age, income, and education were significant factors demonstrates the importance of access to the political system. Access, within this study, is one of the three prerequisites for political participation and includes factors associated with basic needs such as income, education, mobility, and good health. For example, a lower age increases the likelihood that a person will be physically capable of political activity. Education provides the literacy necessary for understanding and benefiting from politics, income reduces the chance of a preoccupation with survival, and mobility allows one to attend meetings and activities.

An examination of the variables which comprise ethnic identification showed that two variables were significantly related to the degree of political participation among this sample. Those born and raised in the United States were significantly more likely to be active than those born and raised in Mexico. The frequency with which Mexico is visited and recentness of immigration to the United States revealed no significant relationship when compared to political participation. Thus, the two variables related to the country raised in provide an indication of socialization to a political culture. These variables lend validity to the concept that native Mexicans are more likely to maintain political orientations characteristic of Mexico, whereas those born and raised in the United States are affected more by the American political culture. Since Mexico represents a subject political culture and the United States represents a participant political culture, the respondents born and raised in Mexico are less likely to be active than those born and raised in the United States.

In addition, political stimuli, represented by geographical location, are important factors in a sense of involvement necessary for participation. In this sample, respondents from urban areas and living in the politically active East and West sides of San Jose were significantly more active. New Mexicans were also found to be more active than those from other states. Political efficacy and sense of citizen duty are also significantly related to political participation. Fifty-eight percent of the actives versus 9 percent of the nonactives felt politically efficacious (a score of three or higher), and 50 percent of the actives versus 11 percent of the nonactives had a sense of citizen duty (a score of three or higher).

Part II: Attitudinal Characteristics of the Politically Active

Political attitudes are examined in relation to several areas, specifically Hispanic politics, generational conflicts, and senior affairs. The study established these parameters because they would be most likely to reveal any alienation among the older Hispanics. Although the data show that disagreement with Hispanic politics and with the Hispanic political movement is not as widespread as originally thought, the study must still thoroughly examine the feelings that the elderly hold on these issues. This examination should uncover whether the views expressed by the aggregate in this sample are the same views held by the politically active and inactive or whether the active have particular views different from those of the inactive. But first we shall see how the respondents' attitudes relate to their actual participation.

Attitudinal linkages to actual participation

The data supported the notion that attitudes reflect participation. In other words, those who stated they would or should participate in Hispanic politics or senior activities were those most likely to do so. The respondents were asked, "Would you join an organization designed to do more for older people?" Table 32 shows that a significant number of the politically active said they would.

A significant relationship also existed between those who said they would join and high rates of past political participation (see Table 33).

Further reinforcement of the link between attitudes and actual behavior arose when the respondents were asked what strategies they would use to solve problems facing the older Hispanic. This

118

TABLE 32

CURRENT POLITICAL PARTICIPATION AND WILLINGNESS
TO JOIN AN ORGANIZATION
(N=70)

| Current Political Participation | Would You Join An Organization? | | | |
| | Yes | | No | |
	N	%	N	%
Nonactive (N=52)	19	37	33	63
Active (N=18)	14	78	4	22

X^2 = 9.126, p < .003.

TABLE 33

PAST POLITICAL PARTICIPATION AND WILLINGNESS
TO JOIN AN ORGANIZATION
(N=68)

| Past Political Participation | Would You Join An Organization? | | | |
| | Yes | | No | |
	N	%	N	%
Nonactive (N=53)	21	40	32	60
Active (N=15)	12	80	3	20

X^2 = 7.631, p < .006.

119

question allowed the respondents to place the responsibility for solutions either on themselves or on outside support systems such as the government, the family, or the church. Among 18 actives, 13 (72 percent) replied that political action and advocacy were needed. Among the nonactives, 15 (39 percent) cited these two political strategies (N = 38). Only two (11 percent) of the actives chose governmental (social services) or traditional support systems (family) as the method for solving these problems, while 17 (45 percent) of the nonactives chose these strategies. These findings show a strong trend for those who are politically active to state strategies based on political action and advocacy, while the inactives' trend is to choose strategies based on assistance from the government and dependence on traditional support systems. Therefore, attitudes expressed by this sample appear significantly related to the extent and nature of their actual participation.

Hispanic politics

Actives and nonactives differ in their attitudes toward Hispanic politics. For example, when asked why they feel the Hispanic elderly are not involved in the "Hispanic political movement," seven (29 percent) of 24 actives on the index of current participation felt the elderly did not participate because of the lack of communication with younger Hispanics and six (25 percent) felt it was due to ideological disagreement. Another five (21 percent) felt it was due to generational conflicts, and the remaining six were evenly divided among responses associated with negative role expectations, fear, and poor self-image. In contrast, 12 (28 percent) of the 43 nonactives felt it was due to negative role expectations and another 12 (28 percent) felt it was due to a lack of communication. However, only eight (19 percent) nonactives stated ideological disagreements and generational conflicts in contrast to 11 (46 percent) actives (N = 24). Therefore, the nonactives apparently believe that generational conflicts and ideological disagreements are not major reasons for inactivity by older Hispanics in Hispanic politics. Instead, a lack of communication and negative role expectations are cited as major reasons. On the other hand, the actives perceive generational conflicts and ideological disagreements to be important reasons; however, this belief did not inhibit their support of Hispanic

politics.   Table   34 shows a statistically significant
relationship between those who rated medium and high on
attitudinal support for Hispanic politics and those who
were   active   on   the   Index   of   Current   Political
Participation.

TABLE 34

INDEX OF ATTITUDINAL SUPPORT FOR HISPANIC
POLITICS BY ACTIVES
(N=67)

Current Political Participation	Low		Medium		High	
	N	%	N	%	N	%
Nonactive (N=44)	18	41	13	30	13	30
Active (N=23)	2	9	8	35	13	57

x^2 = 8.215, p < .017

Generational conflicts

Actives   and   nonactives   showed   no   significant
differences   in   their   attitudes   toward   generational
conflicts.   For   example, when asked if they felt that
Hispanic activists and leaders were dealing with issues
important to them, 11 (52 percent) of   the   21   actives
said   yes   and   10   (48 percent) said no. Among the 40
nonactives,   12   (30   percent)   said   yes   and   28   (70
percent) said no (p < .087). However, both the actives
and   nonactives   agreed   that   younger Hispanics do not
really understand older Hispanics (73 percent   of   both
actives and nonactives).

In   general,   no   significant   relationships   were
found   among   either   the   actives   or   nonactives   in
expressing   a   particular   set   of   attitudes   toward
generational conflicts. Thus,   generational   conflicts
do   not   seem   to   influence   their   amount   of
participation. These findings   also   show   a   lack   of
major   generational   conflicts   and   no strong negative
feelings toward younger Hispanics.

121

Senior citizen issues

In general, more actives than nonactives supported the idea of older Hispanics' participating in age related activities. When asked, "There is a Mexican-American senior citizen club in the East side. They are trying to bring together older people so they can get to know each other. Do you agree that they should?" 91 percent of the actives and 76 percent of the nonactives agreed (p < .116). This indication of support for involvement by older Hispanics in age related activities was reinforced when the index of attitudinal support for senior activities was cross-tabulated with current political participation. Table 35 shows a positive relationship between those who rated medium and high on the index of attitudinal support and those who were active on the index of participation. The frequency distribution shows a strong tendency for the actives to rate medium and high on attitudinal support.

TABLE 35

INDEX OF ATTITUDINAL SUPPORT FOR SENIOR
ACTIVITIES BY ACTIVES
(N=57)

Current Political Participation	Low		Medium		High	
	N	%	N	%	N	%
Nonactive (N=38)	19	50	3	8	16	42
Active (N=19)	7	37	4	21	8	42

X^2 = 2.266, P < .322.

Actives who were members of senior clubs strongly supported age related activities. Thirty-three percent of 24 actives versus 8 percent of 80 nonactives were members of clubs (X^2 = 10.576, p < .002). The actives were also significantly more likely to support involvement with Whites. When asked, "If Anglos were involved in this group (an Hispanic senior citizen club) would you still join," 58 percent of the actives versus 27 percent of the nonactives said yes (X^2 =

5.103, p < .025).

Summary

This sample's attitudes toward political issues
are positively related to political participation;
those who say they will or should participate are more
likely to do so. For example, 78 percent of the
actives versus 37 percent of the nonactives stated they
would join an organization designed to assist older
persons. The actives and nonactives, in terms of
attitudes toward Hispanic politics, both cited a lack
of communication as the major reason for noninvolvement
by Hispanic elderly in Hispanic politics, although the
actives were much more likely to consider generational
conflicts and ideological disagreements as other
important reasons for noninvolvement than the
nonactives (46 percent of actives versus 17 percent
nonactives). However, the actives were significantly
more likely to support Hispanic politics; 57 percent of
the actives versus 30 percent of the nonactives rated
high on an index of attitudinal support for Hispanic
politics. Generational conflicts did not appear to
either discourage or encourage Hispanic elderly to
support or participate in Hispanic politics, although
73 percent of the actives and 73 percent of the
nonactives felt that the younger Hispanic did not
really understand the older Hispanics.

In terms of senior affairs, the actives were more
likely to support involvement by older Hispanics in
age related activities, to be members of senior clubs,
and to support participation with White elderly. For
example, 33 percent of the actives versus 8 percent of
the nonactives were members, and 58 percent of the
actives versus 27 percent of the nonactives stated they
would join a club with White elderly.

Summary and Interpretation

An examination of the characteristics of the
politically active and nonactive shows that they
possessed the following characteristics:

1. The actives generally had incomes of at least
   $4,000.

2. The actives tended to be between 50 and 65
   years old.

3. The actives tended to have 1-12 years of education.

4. The actives were generally born and raised in the United States.

5. The nonactives were generally born and raised in Mexico.

6. The actives were more likely to be raised in urban areas, come from New Mexico, and currently reside in the East and West sides of San Jose.

7. The actives and nonactives both cited a lack of communication (nonactives also cited negative role expectations with equal frequency) as the major reason for noninvolvement by Hispanic elderly in Hispanic politics.

8. The actives were more likely to perceive generational conflicts and ideological disagreements as reasons for noninvolvement by older Hispanics in Hispanic politics than the nonactives.

9. The actives were also significantly more likely to support Hispanic politics than were the nonactives.

10. The actives had significantly higher levels of efficacy and sense of citizen duty than the nonactives.

11. The actives were more likely to support elderly Hispanic involvement in age related activities and were significantly more likely to support participation by older Hispanics with White elderly.

12. The actives were significantly more likely to be members of senior clubs than the nonactives.

Sufficient motivation for participation in political activities depends on a sense of involvement in the political system and in specific issues (Hispanic politics and senior activities), a sense of efficacy, and access to the political structures and processes. Among this sample, the actives usually meet these three criteria. The greater degree of political participation among the actives, in itself, is a significant indicator of a sense of involvement in the political system.

The data also reveal that the actives had a sense of involvement in specific issues such as Hispanic politics and senior activities. The actives were more likely than the nonactives to support Hispanic politics although the level of support by nonactives was also substantial. In addition, the fact that generational conflicts and ideological disagreements did not significantly relate to political participation among either the actives or nonactives further militates against the following two hypotheses: that because of discouragement (generational conflicts) by younger Hispanics the level of participation for older Hispanics will be low in Hispanic politics, and that because of ideological disagreement with the "Hispanic movement" older Hispanics will express negative attitudes toward Hispanic politics. However, most of the sample are not currently active in Hispanic politics. Actives tended to feel generational conflicts and ideological disagreements were major reasons, whereas the nonactive felt it was due to negative role expectations and a lack of communication.

An unexpected, but important, finding was that age consciousness exists among a large portion of the sample, as evidenced by the large number (91 percent of actives, 76 percent of nonactives) who supported older Hispanics organizing through senior clubs. The actives supported participation by older Hispanics in age-related activities and were significantly more likely than nonactives to be members of senior clubs. The greater political acculturation among actives is witnessed by the significantly greater support for involvement with White elderly. This support suggests that the actives recognize the need to work with other groups sharing common problems.

Furthermore, the actives were significantly more likely than nonactives to feel politically efficacious and have a sense of citizen duty. Thus, the hypothesis that those who rank low on political efficacy and a sense of citizen duty will be politically alienated and will manifest such alienation through low rates of political participation is supported.

The examination of the characteristics which differentiate the politically active from the nonactive reveals several factors significantly related to the political acculturation and hence political performance of the actives. Political acculturation to a participant political culture depends on the number of positive political stimuli experienced by a person. A review of the literature found that certain socializing agents such as the school system, combined with historical effects such as discrimination, tend to reinforce subject political orientations and discourage participation. This study's findings indicate that the actives had encountered positive political stimuli. For example, those born and raised in the United States were significantly more likely to be active. Thus, the respondents who grew up in this country apparently had greater opportunities to be exposed to participant politics. The finding that New Mexicans tended to be most active corroborates this. Since New Mexico has always had a political climate that permitted participation by its Hispanic citizens, evidently no incongruency between a subject and a participant political culture existed. In effect, the older persons from New Mexico were raised in a participant political culture. Since New Mexicans are noted for both their strong cultural heritage and their skill in the art of American politics, New Mexico's political climate demonstrates the acculturation of an Hispanic population without subsequent assimilation. The effect of positive political stimuli is also evident in the finding that those from the politically active East and West sides are more likely to participate than those from the politically inactive Park area.

The significantly higher levels of income and education and the lower age among the actives as well as the numerous references to the lack of communication among both actives and nonactives are important indicators that access is important to participation. Significantly greater numbers of actives had incomes over $4,000. Maslow's motivational theory may explain this; before active participation can occur, the basic physical needs must be met. Having sufficient income to meet basic needs reduces the likelihood that survival will preoccupy an older person. Also, the actives were more likely to have a high school education and be between 50 and 65 years. A high school education provides the literacy needed to be politically aware and a younger age decreases the likelihood that physical immobility and poor health

126

will impair participation. Moreover, many older persons considered the lack of communication between younger Hispanics and older Hispanics an important factor. Communication can be considered important to access because one must know what is occurring and how to become involved before one can participate. Many older persons in this sample stated that they did not know what was occurring in Hispanic politics and that no efforts were made to inform them. Thus, communication is important if the older person is to have access to the political system or Hispanic politics.

In summary, the actives demonstrated greater motivation to participate than the nonactives. Higher rates of political activity, a sense of involvement in Hispanic issues and age related activities, a sense of efficacy, and greater access all combined to reveal this. The nonactive manifested their lack of motivation through negative attitudes reflecting alienation from Hispanic politics and senior activities, lower rates of efficacy and political activity, and less access.

1. See Appendix B for comments on the geographical locations of the East side, West side, and Park area.

2. See D.T. Valdes, "A Political History of New Mexico," mimeographed document, Denver, Colorado, Revised 1971, p.4, and J. Holmes, Politics in New Mexico (Albuquerque: University of New Mexico Press, 1967), for information on New Mexico politics.

3. The scales on political efficacy and citizen duty are Guttman scales. As such, the optimum validity level for the coefficient of reproducibility is .9 or higher, and for the coefficient of scalability it is a coefficient above .6 if the scales are to be truly unidimensional and cumulative (see N. Nie; D. Bent; and H. Hull, Statistical Package for the Social Sciences (SPSS) (New York: McGraw-Hill, 1970), pp. 196-207). Although the coefficient of reproducibility (.8333) and coefficient of scalability (.5522) for the efficacy scale and for the citizen duty scale (reproducibility = .8529, scalability = .5652) is slightly below the optimal levels, they are relatively close, therefore, the scales are considered valid for this study.

CHAPTER V

ANALYSIS OF PERSONAL EXPERIENCES

This chapter will study personal experiences which influenced the attitudes of the respondents toward politics and government. Examining the personal experiences of selected respondents serves several purposes: (1) it depicts the historical events in the older person's life that affected his political outlook, (2) it reveals the older person's reactions in the face of a politically insecure environment, and (3) it makes the study findings previously presented more personal. Using personal experiences in examining political behavior is important because the experiences are integral to acculturation to a political culture. Pye and Verba (1965) state that a person draws inferences about the nature of a political process from personal experiences with a political system. These inferences then become part of the individual's political belief system (attitudes) and lead to evaluations applied to new situations.

A review of the political history of Hispanics in this country revealed that political suppression, poverty, and discrimination existed to the extent that Hispanics were discouraged from participating in politics. This sample was asked: "We are interested in the ways the events of a person's life influence the way he acts about politics and government. Can you remember any event that had an effect on how you feel about politics and government in this country or in Mexico? Are there any experiences in your life that changed your views about politics or about participating in politics?" Forty-six persons responded, giving extra time to the interviewer.[1]
Their responses and experiences were varied; no two had had the same experience. Therefore the experiences they related were categorized under three broad classifications: discrimination, poverty, and revolution. Since some respondents dealt with two or three separate classifications, extra categories were added to account for these: poverty and discrimination, and discrimination, poverty, and revolution. For example, if a respondent recounted separate incidents of discrimination and poverty, he was classified under the category of

discrimination/poverty. In general, the responses show that the sample experienced many of the events characteristic of their age cohort (see Table 36).[2]

TABLE 36

EXPERIENCES OF RESPONDENTS
(N=46)

Experience	Number
Revolution	1
Discrimination	19
Poverty	4
Poverty and Discrimination	17
Discrimination, poverty, and revolution	5

Table 36 shows that 17 of the 46 respondents mentioned experiences of discrimination and poverty which had some influence on their political attitudes. The greatest number (19) mentioned incidents of discrimination only, while five mentioned incidents associated with all three. The most common experience dealt with discrimination and racism. More than any other experiences, these had the greatest effect on the older persons' current attitudes toward politics and toward Whites in general. For example, Senora R, 64 years old, was born and raised in Texas. She remembers how Mexicans "were shot down like dogs" ("lo mataron como perros") by White ranchers. She states that, to this day, she is still filled with bitterness toward the discrimination she saw in Texas. Senor J, 70 years old, is also from Texas. He recalls that one day, when he was young, he had gone into a store to buy ice cream. After collecting the young boy's money, the owner, an Anglo, promptly threw the ice cream into the street. A fuller description of discrimination and prejudice was given by Senor U.

Senor U was born in Mexico in 1907. In 1919 he crossed the border into the United States to find work. In the 1930s he found himself working in the fields of Arizona. During this period he was witness to the "massacres" of union members during several strikes

130

occurring at that time. He states he was
never directly involved, although at one time
he was arrested by the police during a
strike. He eventually migrated to
California, looking for work in the grape
fields of Southern California. One day, he
and his family were arriving from Mexicali, a
border town in Mexico, to Westmoreland, a
small town in the Calexico Valley. The Border
Patrol stopped their car for an apparently
routine search for illegal aliens. Since
Senor U is not a citizen, he carries his
birth certificate in case he should be
stopped. When the border patrolman asked for
their papers and Senor U presented his, the
patrolman grasped the certificate, rubbed it
on his behind, threw it to the ground, and
told Senor U: "This is what they're good
for." Several months ago Senor U's son was
beaten by police in what Senor U considers an
unprovoked assault. Naturally, because of
these events, Senor U holds a great deal of
resentment toward Whites and toward the
police.

Such incidents of discrimination yielded distrust
and bitterness toward Whites in general. Many
respondents continued to express their resentments
toward Whites for the racism they encountered many
years before. In one case, this bitterness was
exemplified in an incident "proudly" recounted by Senor
L.

Senor L is 59 years old, very articulate,
friendly and relatively active in community
affairs. He lives in the older part of the
East side barrio and is proud to have lived
in the same house for over 25 years. He was
born and raised in Northern New Mexico. Like
many other New Mexicans, his family and his
father were involved in politics. He says
that when he was 10 years old living in
Northern New Mexico, no "Gringos" (Whites)
lived in the area. In this particular part
of New Mexico Chicanos owned most, if not
all, of the land and would shoot any Whites
who came into the area -- especially Texans,
who were particularly hated. Even the old
men were not exempt from this type of
action. One night, two Whites had stopped by

131

the Rio Grande to cook and camp out. Two old Mexicans were waiting in hiding and shot them as they were lighting their fires. The old men then proceeded to throw the bodies into the Rio Grande. When some other Chicanos came along to ask what had happened, the old men responded: "Se fueron con el rio!" ("They went with the river").

Senor L is especially bitter about the land they lost. His family owned land in New Mexico; but the state government, during the Depression, instituted a tax that most Chicanos could not afford. Their land was then forfeited and sold to a wealthy White man who later resold it at a substantial profit. Senor L's father attempted to organize other Chicanos to prevent their lands from being taken away. However, he was unsuccessful, and Senor L's family eventually moved to California to find work.

The respondents described many situations involving poverty. In many cases, poverty overlapped with discrimination in affecting the older persons's attitudes toward politics. Poverty was, and continues to be, the normal economic state for most older Hispanics. It has affected the political awareness and political participation of most Hispanic elderly. To some, it has accentuated the injustice of their socioeconomic condition and has promoted their political action. To most others, it has discouraged active participation because of their intense struggle for survival. Senor S is one of the few who has realized the need to organize politically to improve living conditions and eliminate discrimination.

Senor S is 63 years old and was born in the northern state of Sonora, Mexico. He remembers that because of the extreme poverty there, his father did not want him to grow up poor; so he was sent to live with relatives in California. He entered the state illegally and was almost caught by the Border Patrol. When he lived in Mexico, he thought life would be good in the United States. However, he quickly changed his mind once he spent time in this country. The police harassed him and called him derogatory names. He eventually wound up working in the fields, where he saw much discrimination and poverty. Although he did not like what he saw, he felt that if he complained he would be sent back to Mexico. After he married a woman from this country, he felt more secure in voicing his grievances. He attempted to organize a union in the 1950s with the aid of organizers. He was arrested and blacklisted. Therefore he became a janitor. Although he was bitter because the White labor organizers left the workers alone when the police came, he says that the experience and his desire to help his people only made him more determined to stay active.

Senora M told a different story but with a similar outcome.

Senora M is 65 years old, comes from New Mexico, and lives in the West side. She was married at a young age and spent her time raising a family and occasionally worked part time to help her husband. About 10 years ago her husband became sick and died. She then had to work full time in the canneries to support her family. After her children were married and left home, she became active in senior citizen activities. Although she had never been involved in organizations during her life, she felt that in her old age she would finally have the time to be involved in community issues. She has been active in Model Cities and the Community Services Organization (CSO) as well as senior clubs.

Many respondents never escaped the cycle of poverty. In their old age they have begun to feel that their lives were spent in an economic system that neither rewarded them sufficiently for their productivity nor remembered them in their later years. Senor P is one older person who feels he has been exploited.

Senor P is 69 years old and lives in the Park area with his wife. He has lived in San Jose for 20 years and has four children. For 18 years Senor P worked in a fruit and vegetable cannery in San Jose. He is now completely disabled and very bitter that he left his life in the canneries ("deje mi vida con la

133

caneria") with nothing to show for it. He used to get hurt at work but was afraid to say anything because he might get laid off. He became especially angry when his son applied for a job at the same cannery and, despite his personal requests to a foreman he knew to allow his son to work, was turned down.

Several respondents described their experiences during the Mexican Revolution. These descriptions illustrate the combined effects of discrimination, poverty, and a revolution on political behavior.

Senor E is 71 years old and has lived in the East side with his family for 38 years. They bought the house they live in and own a few houses nearby. He has his own garden, grows his own vegetables and flowers, and sells roses to supplement his income. In addition to being self-sufficient, he is politically aware and active. He strongly supports the UFW and is involved in community activities.

Senor E was born and raised in the state of Michoacan, Mexico. When he was young, his family worked for an hacendado (landowner). During harvest time the patron's (boss's) men would constantly be looking over the workers's shoulders to make sure they did not steal corn for their families. Senor E recalls that their position was hopeless because they could not go anywhere else; if they had they would only be in the same situation with another patron.

When the Revolution occurred, Senor E was 18. He did not participate, but many others whom he knew joined with Villa. He feels the poor were justified in joining Villa because life was so hard for them. To avoid the chaos and dangers of the Revolution, his father and family fled to the United States. Three days after crossing the border, his father was killed in an accident. Senor E states that from the time of the Revolution he has been interested in politics; primarily because of these experiences, he has supported the poor and oppressed.

Senora W also lived through the Mexican Revolution
but, unlike Senor E, became politically cynical and
inactive.

> Senora W is 81 years old. She is widowed and
> lives alone. She came to the United States
> at the height of the Mexican Revolution. She
> remembers that young girls would have to be
> hidden whenever federal troops and guerrillas
> arrived. Her family owned land at the time
> of the Revolution but lost most of it. To
> this day she decries the violence and
> bloodshed that occurred. To escape the
> Revolution, her family crossed the border at
> night. She married and settled down in San
> Jose. She is very religious and believes her
> family is all-important. She disagrees
> vehemently with militant Mexican-Americans
> and feels they should be grateful for what
> they have in this country.

Although most experiences recounted by the
respondents dealt with negative incidents related to
discrimination, poverty, and revolution, certain
positive incidents encouraged some respondents to
become aware and involved. Several of these
experiences concerned the Roosevelt era and the work of
Cesar Chavez and Father McDonald in San Jose. For
example, some respondents cited Roosevelt and the New
Deal as the reasons for their lifelong affiliation with
the Democratic party.

> Senora C, although 72 years old, remains
> politically aware. She strongly supports the
> UFW. She appears knowledgeable about the
> Hispanic political movement and generally
> supports it. She stated that she did not
> become politically interested until the time
> of the Roosevelt administration when she saw
> how poor people were being helped. Because
> of the Roosevelt administration, she
> registered as a Democrat and began to vote.

On the other hand, Senor F, who is 82 and has
lived in the East side for years, did not
become politically active until the 1950s.
At that time Cesar Chavez was organizing
Mexican-Americans under the auspices of the
Community Services Organization (CSO). He
remembers Cesar well. Cesar taught night

courses in a local school and was Senor F's wife's teacher. Cesar also encouraged Senor F to participate in the CSO, which at that time spearheaded political issues in the barrios of San Jose. Senor F remained an active member of CSO until several years ago when he became too ill to attend meetings.

The experiences recounted above demonstrate that not all reacted the same way. Although some became politically active and aware, many became cynical and afraid. Several broad categories were established to include the various reactions to the experiences with discrimination, poverty and revolution. These categories are defined by whether the reactions were "active" (becoming involved, opposing a situation, or resolving a situation), "fearful" (becoming afraid, inactive, or cynical), or "fatalistic" (accepting and rationalizing an incident as something uncontrollable, bound to be suffered, or unimportant because of its common occurence). A fourth category, "passive," includes those who did not actively oppose an incident but passively resented it or became more sympathetic to others who actively sought to oppose the particular incident (see Table 37). Twenty-two of the 44 respondents fell into the active category, eight each in the fatalistic and fear category, and six in the passive category. Examining these reactions provides a greater understanding of why some older persons continue to practice a politics of deference, while others practice a politics of competition and confrontation.

TABLE 37

RESPONDENTS' REACTIONS TO DISCRIMINATION, POVERTY AND REVOLUTION (N=44)

Reaction	Number
Active	22
Fear	8
Fatalistic	8
Passive	6

Several older Hispanics reacted positively to their political experiences. Some acted passively in sympathy with others who were active opponents to the political situation. For example, Senora C, described earlier as the woman who joined the Democratic party during the Roosevelt era, has experienced discrimination in Texas and feels that discrimination still exists in California. However, although she is not an active participant in political issues, she continues to vote as a Democrat, supports the UFW, and is a member of the Libertad Club. Another example is Senor B.

Senor B is 72 years old, lives in the East side, and is very poor. He grew up in Colorado and came to California 40 years ago. He has been poor all his life and has accepted his fate as one of God's wishes. Nonetheless, he is politically interested in Chicano politics and supports the UFW and the Hispanic political movement. Although he considers himself physically incapable of active participation, he does what he can to support Chicanos. For example, he has on occasion attempted to convince other senior friends to support specific Chicano community issues. He himself will not cross a UFW picket line at a local supermarket, even if he must waste a shopping trip. His family is also politically involved. His daughter pickets for the Union, and his son-in-law is politically active. Interestingly, he refuses to join the Libertad Club because he feels it is not a politically active organization.

These two respondents are examples of older Hispanics who, because of negative experiences such as discrimination and poverty, at least understand why Hispanics' political actions are needed, even though they are not active. However, some respondents became active either in spite of or because of their political experiences. Senor S, for example, became active in unions after his encounters with the police. Senor E and Senor L also became active and remain active in their old age.

Because of his experiences during the Mexican Revolution, Senor E has remained interested in politics and community issues. Although

137

he does not participate in formal
organizations, he does "defend" himself and
others whenever necessary. At times he also
participates in group actions. For example,
several friends and neighbors complained that
the Department of Motor Vehicles
discriminated against them because they could
not speak English and the Department refused
to hire interpreters. Senor E rounded up
these people and several supporters, went to
the Department, and lodged a loud and public
protest.

Senor L, who recounted the story about the
"Gringos" on the Rio Grande, moved to
California after his family lost their land
in New Mexico. Despite their poverty and
their need to work hard, he and his wife
remained active in community affairs. His
wife is currently a registrar in the East
side. He actively participated in a local
Hispanics' political campaign for a city
council seat. Senor L and his wife are also
members of the Libertad Club, where he is a
member of the group's Mexican band.

Those with "active" reactions to their experiences
also rated active on the index of current political
participation. When the categories of reactions were
cross-tabulated with the index of current political
participation, all but two of the 16 actives on the
index reacted actively to their experiences (X^2 =
14.618, p < .003) (see Table 38).

In addition, the active respondents stated strong
support for Hispanic politics and senior activities.
For example, Senor E states: "All older Hispanics
should get together in senior citizen groups because it
is not good to be alone when one is old." Senora S, who
supports Hispanic activists, states: "En varias maneras
estan (los Mexicanos) contra la discriminacion y es la
misma cosa que afecta a los viejos" ("The
Mexican-Americans are against the same discrimination
that affect the older people"). This is consistent
with the findings in Chapter IV that the actives are
more likely than the nonactives to support Hispanic
politics and age related activities.

138

TABLE 38

CURRENT POLITICAL PARTICIPATION AND RESPONDENTS'
REACTIONS TO EXPERIENCES
(N=44)

Current Political Participation	Active		Fear		Fatalistic		Passive	
	N	%	N	%	N	%	N	%
Nonactive (N=28)	8	28	8	28	7	25	5	18
Active (N=16)	14	88	0	0	1	6	1	6

X^2 = 14.618, p < .003.

In general, the respondents who reacted actively had one thing in common: they perceived their situation as unacceptable and resolved to do something about it. The majority, however, may have recognized the injustice of their situation but did not actively or passively oppose it. Instead, some became cynical or afraid, and others became "fatalistic." Those termed fatalistic and fearful are characterized by their deference to authority figures and to the political system, particularly local and state. They acquiesce, do not demand change, and try to cope with only their situation. For example, Senora W., whose family fled the Mexican Revolution, can be considered an older person who practices a politics of deference. She is wary about politics. She feels that life is much better in this country, and although Mexicans are still poor and discriminated against, they should be grateful for what they have. As her children were growing up, she cautioned them not to become involved in politics; and after her family settled in this country, found jobs, and married, she attended night school until she successfully passed her citizenship test.

Another manifestation of a politics of deference is religiosity. Generally, it appeared that the more religious the respondent, the less his political activity.

Senor F is 68 years old and was born and raised in Mexico. He and his wife became

139

very religious approximately eight years
ago. He converted to the Apostolic faith
because he felt there was too much injustice
in this world. He experienced discrimination
when he was younger but feels he has now
found peace. He states that "I never get
involved; I mind my own business. It is
better that one should practice his religion
and not bother others ... only though God
will one find faith and salvation."

Perhaps more typical of respondents who practice a
politics of deference are those who simply stay out of
politics and adhere to their traditional roles. The
female is more likely to do this. She may value her
role as wife and mother and may not feel that she has
the time or that she has a right to participate in
politics.

Senora Z is 69 years old and was born in
Mexico. She comes from a large family and
during the Depression moved to California.
She feels that the Mexican woman should be
mother and wife and deplores girls'
liberalness. She has never been involved in
politics because it is not her function. She
states that had she wanted to be involved,
her husband would not have let her. She says
that "Women are not raised to be involved, it
is not their function."

Some respondents reacted very differently.
Instead of becoming active or fatalistic, they became
cynical or afraid. Because of experiences with
political suppression they view politics as threatening
and something to be avoided.

Senora Y is 78 years old. She was born in
Zacatecas, Mexico, and lived there until
1953, when she came to the United States.
When she was younger and living in Mexico,
she experienced an incident which, as she
says, "frightened her out of politics." In
Zacatecas there existed a great deal of
corruption. Shortly before she came to the
United States, a state election was held and
an unpopular candidate was elected governor.
The people were angry and demanded a recount,
but the ballots had been stolen. The women
of her pueblo organized a protest. However,

during this protest, the corrupt candidate created a confrontation, and three male supporters with the women were killed. The women were blamed and several were arrested. Senora Y managed to escape from her pueblo and eventually entered the United States. She does not now participate in any Hispanic issues and generally refuses to discuss political issues. Only after assurances that her name would not be disclosed would she recount the incident to the interviewer.

Senor X did not have a dramatic experience as did Senora Y. However, the effects of his experience were still the same: he is afraid to be politically involved.

Senor X is 65, from Jalisco, Mexico, and lives in the East side. His family was very poor; so in 1927 they entered the United States in search of work. Senor X was fortunate to become a plumber's apprentice. He learned well, became a plumber, and created a comfortable life for himself and his family. He is proud that he is a "self-made" man but realizes that his success is an exception to that of most Hispanics who came to this country. Politically he is conservative and strongly disapproves of the Hispanic political movement and its militancy. He also feels that "elderly Hispanics have no right getting involved in politics. They are being used if they do get into militant activity." The interview revealed that he did not want to jeopardize his position as a plumber. He feels that if he becomes actively involved in Hispanic politics, it will jeopardize his pension and his position in the plumbers' union.

Several respondents specifically mentioned that they were afraid to be involved because they might get deported.

Senor G is 64 years old and from the state of Coahuila, Mexico. He came to the United States in 1942 under the Bracero Program. This program allowed Mexican nationals to work in the United States for a limited period. However, many braceros remained in the United States illegally; Senor G was one such person. He worked several years as a bracero and remembers being cheated out of his wages. He wanted to complain but was told that if he did, he would be sent back to Mexico. After a time he left the fields for the cities, married, and raised a family. Since his farm labor days he has felt that he is in this country only "through the grace of God." Therefore, because he does not want to be deported, he avoids politics and community activities.

The respondents' experiences show that discrimination, poverty, and revolution affected their attitudes about politics and government. But not all reacted in the same manner. Some became active and aware, others accepted the situation as inevitable or unavoidable, and still others became cynical and afraid. Nonetheless, they all had one reaction in common: negative feelings toward politics in general and toward Whites and the police in particular. Although the descriptions presented in this chapter account for only 43 percent of the sample, they do give a strong indication that older Hispanics experienced events characteristic of their age cohort. Most of the total sample is inactive, and most of the limited sample in this chapter recounted negative events and negative feelings about politics. Therefore, both the data and the respondents' personal experiences support the hypothesis <u>that</u> <u>those</u> <u>who</u> <u>are</u> <u>found</u> <u>to</u> <u>have</u> <u>negative</u> <u>experiences</u> <u>in politics</u> <u>during</u> <u>their</u> <u>lifetime</u> <u>will</u> <u>express</u> <u>negative</u> <u>feelings</u> <u>about</u> <u>participation</u> <u>in</u> <u>politics</u>.

1.   Because of the length of the interview not all were able or willing to expand the extra hour or two needed for this section.

2.   Corridos, or tales, are popular forms of recounting stories of adventures, heroism, romance and injustices encountered by Hispanics, particularly in parts of the Southwest (Texas, New Mexico, Arizona) and Northern Mexico.   Corridos are generally songs with a story and usually recount an incident, plot, or event that occurred. Many of them relate to the period in the early Twentieth century, particularly the period of the Mexican revolution and the period 1900-1930.   One example of a corrido which occurred during the formative period of today's elder cohort who emigrated from Texas is the "Corrido of Gregorio Cortez", which recounts a shooting in which Gregorio Cortez is accused of murdering a sheriff and two members of a posse. The corrido relates the discrimination experienced by Hispanics in Texas, Cortez's attempts to protect himself and his family, his trial and subsequent imprisonment.   This corrido is now popularized in a film.

CHAPTER VI

SUMMARY, IMPLICATIONS, AND CONCLUSIONS

Thus far, the study has investigated the political attitudes and political participation of the Hispanic elderly. A survey of 106 elderly Hispanics residing in San Jose has revealed various political activities and attitudes. This chapter will summarize the findings from the survey, interpret the findings, draw implications, and provide conclusions.

A review of the literature revealed several conceptual models that might help one understand the older Hispanics' political behavior in relation to their social, economic, cultural, and political background. The theories of political culture and political socialization indicate that the political orientations and attitudes of elderly Hispanics are affected by socializing agents characteristic of a mixed political culture. In addition, historical developments in the age cohort and the older persons' lack of access to the political structures and processes decreases both their ability and their desire to participate in politics. Consideration of these concepts and issues suggested that the older Hispanic would practice a politics of deference, manifested by a limited sense of involvement in the political system and in Hispanic politics, a feeling of political inefficacy, and substantial problems with access. To test the extent to which these expectations would apply to the sample, five hypotheses were developed. The data supported three of them:

1. That because of their social, economic, cultural, and political position, the elderly Hispanics will be found to cluster near the low end of the hierarchy of political involvement (apathetic, least active).

2. That those who rank low in a sense of political efficacy and citizen duty will be politically alienated and will show such alienation through low rates of political participation.

3. That those with negative experiences in politics during their lifetime will express negative feelings about participation in

145

politics.

The data did not support two hypotheses:

4. That because of discouragement (generational conflicts) by younger Hispanics, the level of participation in Hispanic politics for older Hispanics will be low.

5. That because of ideological disagreement with the "Hispanic political movement," older Hispanics will express negative attitudes toward Hispanic politics.

The research task had three primary objectives: to examine political activity, to assess attitudes, and to study the sources of variation.

Summary of Findings

Levels of political activity

Older Hispanics were found to be relatively inactive in overall participation; however, political activity was higher than expected. The elderly Hispanics in the sample rated favorably on political interest and political awareness. The extensive political and senior-citizen organizing as well as the strong support for Chavez and the UFW in the San Jose barrios partially explain this. Moreover, elderly Hispanics born and raised in the United States were more active than those born and raised in Mexico. The impact of American political orientations stressing civic competence and political participation might explain this.

Twenty to 23 respondents had engaged in political activities (gladiatorial and transitional) during their lifetime. Past political activities had been primarily in Hispanic related politics with many of the actives having engaged in confrontation politics. Those who had participated in Hispanic political activities in the past were significantly more likely to support contemporary Hispanic politics.

Attitudes of older Hispanics

Assessing the attitudes toward specific issue areas -- Hispanic politics, general citizenship, and age related activities -- revealed a dichotomy between

146

the older person's attitudes toward specific issues and his attitudes toward the general arena of politics.

The respondents' personal experiences revealed much bitterness and distrust toward Whites and thus toward politics in general; these politics often being viewed as White-dominated arenas. Many of the older persons had experienced discrimination and poverty and were resentful of the treatment they had received at the hands of the police, politicians, and other authority figures. Nevertheless, attitudinal support for Hispanic political activities and age related activities existed: 39 percent and 42 percent rated high on indices of attitudinal support for Hispanic politics and senior activities, respectively.

Because of generational conflicts and ideological disagreements among older Hispanics, one would not expect them to support Hispanic politics; but support existed among both the nonactives and the actives in the sample, although more so among the actives. That past political activities had focused on Hispanic related politics conforms with the favorable attitudes older persons have toward Hispanic politics. Thus a propensity for those active in past political activities to support current Hispanic politics is evident. But because of fear and a lack of communication, most of the older Hispanics were not currently active in Hispanic related politics. Various respondents stated that Hispanics ignore the elderly, make no efforts to inform them of important issues in the community, and do not encourage them to participate even though the elderly are eager to know more about local community issues and political issues affecting Hispanics throughout the Southwest.

The lack of communication undoubtedly contributes to political alienation and apathy. Yet a lack of communication is also open to change since informing an older person of relevant issues is easier than overcoming psychological factors such as attitudinal disagreement. Although several older persons disliked and disagreed with the Hispanic movement and with certain Hispanic politics, a larger number of the sample stated that more communication between Hispanic leaders and activists and the elderly would enhance the willingness of the elderly to support and become involved in these politics.

Fear is more formidable. Those older Hispanics

who mentioned fear were referring to political involvement's possible negative consequences such as loss of citizenship, loss of Social Security, and deportation. Although fear can discourage older persons from participation, those respondents who are currently afraid to become involved may, through better communication, become more secure in supporting the various political issues concerning their community.

Because of a suspected lack of age-group consciousness and continued adherence to the kinship system, this study speculated that the older persons would not support age related activities. Although few elderly Hispanics actively participated in senior centers, they indicated approval of involvement by older Hispanics in age related activities. Most of the respondents, both active and nonactive, had an age-group consciousness; that is, they realized that older persons have common interests and should participate on a peer-group level rather than on an age-heterogeneous level. However, the actives were more likely to support participation in senior activities and cooperation with White elderly than nonactives; they were also significantly more likely to be members of senior clubs.

The primary reasons given for noninvolvement in senior centers were apathy, poor self-image, and negative role expectations. Nonetheless, the potential for greater involvement in age related activities exists among the sample. For example, if the two categories most amenable to change -- functional capabilities and communication (if transportation were improved, organizing conducted, more information made available) -- were combined, they would comprise 37 percent of all responses. This suggests that among this sample great latitude is available for getting more elderly persons involved in senior activities.

Sources of variation

In general, the respondents who rated active on an index of current political participation had significantly different characteristics from the nonactives. The actives were more likely to support Hispanic politics, age related activities, and participation with White elderly; they were significantly more likely to be members of senior centers. In addition, the actives have higher incomes, have achieved more education, and are younger than the nonactives. Thus, this sample met the three basic criteria important for participation as set out in the conceptual model. They had a greater sense of involvement in the political system, Hispanic politics, and age related activities as well as a greater sense of efficacy and citizen duty. In addition, their access was greater than that of nonactives because their higher income, greater education, and younger age allowed them to meet basic needs, possess the necessary literacy, and be less susceptible to the degenerative effects of old age. Also, the actives were more likely to come from urban areas, live in the politically active East and West sides of San Jose, and have been born and raised in New Mexico.

Another major finding of this study has been the validation of the theoretical contention that incongruency of two political cultures creates serious problems for the group socialized to the less dominant political culture. The sample related various experiences which showed that many older persons realized early in life that political participation is a key to political power in this country. However, respondents born and raised in Mexico and thus more socialized to the Mexican political culture were more likely to be unsure of the political tactics employed in this country, were constantly reminded of their inferior status, and were subjected to negative political stimuli such as discrimination. Therefore, a significantly greater proportion of those born and raised in Mexico were politically inactive; they reflected this through a sense of alienation. Thus, acculturation seems to be a necessary ingredient for political participation. One explanation for this is that knowledge of a system allows for a greater probability for opportunity to participate. Therefore, degree of acculturation provides one source of variation between the actives and nonactives.

Conclusions of Research Findings

This discussion will focus on possible conclusions from the research findings. These conclusions are not the only possible ones which might be drawn from the results of the data analysis, but they do relate to some of the most important issues. While many of the findings in this study were far from conclusive, many of the following conclusions are important components of the political behavior of older Hispanics. In short, although this study, on the basis of one sample, has not indisputably revealed the complex relationships between the older person's political behavior and the effect of his social, political, and cultural environment, it has identified some ideas which could greatly benefit future endeavors.

1. Elderly Hispanics are relatively inactive in politics, but their political awareness and political interest are high.

2. Strong support exists for Hispanic and age related politics, although actual involvement in these areas is not high.

3. The potential for increased involvement by elderly Hispanics in Hispanic and age related activities exists.

4. Greater communication between the young and old may be an important resource for increasing the political awareness and political participation of older Hispanics.

5. A politics of deference has been the primary political tactic for most of the sample and is still practiced by many.

6. Three useful conceptual models for understanding the current political behavior of the older Hispanic are the concepts of political cultures, political socialization, and the politics of deference.

7. A sense of involvement, a sense of efficacy, and access are important factors in motivating older Hispanic persons to participate in politics.

Politics of Deference

In addition to meeting the original three objectives, the exploration of the political behavior among older Hispanics provides the format for understanding why elderly Hispanics practice a politics of deference. Chapter V showed that the personal experiences of the respondents are important factors in understanding their political socialization and political acculturation. Since many respondents experienced discrimination, poverty, and revolution, they withdrew from any political activities which would bring them to the attention of the police, courts, bureaucracies, and other authority figures. Their current attitudes reflect this: "Chicanos should not be militant," "They should be grateful for what they have," or "The family and church are more important than politics." Not all of the respondents, however, submitted to their political situation; some became politically active. Most, however, did not and in their old age counseled a conservative approach to politics.

Younger Hispanics tend to resent such conservatism. Of course, younger Hispanics may not realize that a politics of deference was and continues to seem for many older Hispanics a necessary tool of survival. Younger Hispanics, as much as they may have suffered discrimination and political repression, have not suffered them to the extent the older person has. Many younger Hispanics, at least, have had the advantage of being born and raised and better educated in this country and, as a result, are more acculturated to the American political system. Hence, no matter how severe political repression might have been, the younger Hispanic has had a better opportunity to learn how to use the American system; the Hispanic political gains are good examples of this. Therefore, a younger Hispanic must understand that many older Hispanics are practicing a politics of deference while the younger person is practicing a politics of confrontation and competition. An older person's practice of a politics of deference does not negate his desire for involvement in contemporary Hispanic politics. The attitudinal support toward Hispanic politics among older persons and their sense that communication is lacking clearly suggests that the potential for cooperation between the old and young exists. Political partnership between the young and old around common social, cultural, and political issues could be accomplished in several ways.

Greater communication is one important tool. Communication is directly related to access and a sense of involvement and efficacy. Education classes, contact between the young and old, and greater participation by younger Hispanics in senior centers are examples. The Libertad Senior Center, although a social-recreational club, has invited speakers from the United Farmworkers to present their views. In the same manner older and younger Hispanics could discuss such issues as police brutality and the need for bilingual, bicultural education. A primary resource for communicating community issues to the elderly Hispanic is the church because of the strong religious ties and frequent church attendance of the elderly. Even though the data did not reveal significant relationships between church attendance and political awareness, the church could be used as a tool for community organizing of older persons. The next section discusses the implications of the findings and examines the possible impacts of greater political participation by Hispanic elders.

Implications

The implications of this study focus on three broad areas: The potential for political participation by the Spanish speaking elderly, the impact of such participation and the issues that remain to be addressed in future studies of political behavior among Spanish speaking elderly. Before examining these areas it is useful to examine the historical events of the last decade which are influencing the potential for political participation.

Historical events

The First National Conference on the Spanish-speaking Elderly (Kansas City, March 4-7, 1975) was the first attempt at bringing together individuals interested in the plight of Hispanic elderly. The conference raised three issues especially pertinent to their political position: 1) that the Spanish speaking elderly have not previously been considered a politically interested or aware aging group; 2) that the Spanish speaking elderly currently are politically powerless but have the potential to improve their situation; and 3) that the Spanish speaking elderly are in fact politically aware and desire to be politically influential in age related politics.

The conference, sponsored by the National Chicano Social Planning Council, Cuban Social Planning Council and other Puerto Rican, Cuban and Hispanic groups, was established to bring together Latinos -- young and old, professional and nonprofessional -- interested in the social and political problems of the elderly and in developing an advocacy organization for the Spanish-speaking elderly. The proceedings of the conference amply demonstrated the articulateness and political awareness of the elderly who attended. They

152

were vocal -- even demanding -- in support of the creation of an association dedicated to political objectives. At the conclusion of the conference, participants endorsed the creation of a national organization to advocate for Spanish speaking elderly (Hernandez and Mendoza, 1975).

The findings of this study lend the following empirical evidence to the subjective conclusion of the conference: that Spanish speaking elderly want political representation and political influence in the public policies that affect them. The conference also supported the contention that the politics of the Spanish speaking elderly tend to emphasize cultural nationalism. In other words, the Spanish speaking elderly are interested in political power for the sake of better social services and a voice in government and for the preservation of their cultural heritage through the incorporation of multi-lingual and multi-cultural characteristics in programs and activities. The conference stimulated several important events: the development of aged based organizations for the Hispanic elderly and increased involvement by Hispanic professionals in gerontology and Hispanic seniors in politically oriented activities.

The Asociacion Nacional Pro Personas Mayores (National Association for Spanish speaking elderly), the first nationally based organization designed to advocate for Hispanic elderly, was a direct outgrowth of the 1975 Kansas City Conference. Its formation also was influenced by the lack of Hispanic representation at the 1971 White House Conference on Aging. At that conference, Hispanic participants became concerned with the small number of Hispanic delegates and seniors in attendance and the absence of workshops on Spanish speaking elderly. They joined with Black participants in objecting to those conditions and were successful in creating a special concerns session on Hispanic elderly and incorporating their recommendations in the conference proceedings (Owens, et al., 1973; U.S. Department of Health, Education and Welfare, 1972).

Many of those individuals were instrumental in organizing the 1975 Kansas City Conference and in creating the Asociacion Nacional Pro Personas Mayores. Since its founding, that organization has been successful in increasing funds for research and training in Hispanic aging, promoting representation on

153

peer review panels in the Administration on Aging, supporting expansion of senior programs and drafting regulations and legislation to benefit the Hispanic elderly. By 1977, additional organizations were formed to represent specific Hispanic subgroups--Puerto Rican, Mexican-American and Cuban elderly -- and professional interests. The most prominent of these groups is the National Hispanic Council on Aging, organized to promote participation in gerontology and geriatrics by Hispanic professionals. The work of that council in disseminating information, providing technical assistance and developing a network of professionals and practitioners to assist Hispanic elderly is growing and has a measurable impact on the development of Hispanic gerontology and geriatrics.

Those events represent a separate achievement: the growing interest among Hispanics in gerontology and geriatrics with a resultant increase in the number of Hispanics working to provide services and programs for older Hispanics. With the proliferation of academic courses, university departments and training programs in gerontology, efforts are being made to increase the number of Hispanics acquiring degrees and certificates in those fields. Although it is unknown how many are now working in aging, observation clearly indicates that Hispanics are becoming interested in those areas. More importantly, many of these professionals have become the primary leaders in providing advocacy and political representation for Hispanic elderly. To a large extent, those professionals have largely been responsible for the accomplishments achieved for the Hispanic elderly throughout the 1970s.

There remains, however, an important question: have the elderly themselves provided the leadership? An examination of the individuals providing leadership in advocacy, development of programs and services and advancement of professional and educational interests indicates that the middle-aged and younger cohorts of Hispanics have been more visible than the elderly. Few elderly Hispanics have been active participants in the leadership of the various aged based organizations. More importantly, it appears that none of the organizations have developed a mass membership of Hispanic senior citizens. It is evident that senior citizens are active in church groups, senior citizen clubs and neighborhood activities, but in the larger world of policymaking and state and federal politics, Hispanic seniors have been conspicuously absent. Their absence, however, is not surprising. Developing large-scale organizations and effectively dealing with complex federal and state bureaucracies, legislative bodies and politics requires a certain degree of sophistication, education, energy, time and resources to become involved. As this study indicates, few Hispanic elderly have had that luxury.

The following questions therefore arise: what is the potential for Hispanic elderly to become politically involved in age related political activities? Is this unlikely due to their socioeconomic position, their culture and/or the predominance of professionals? Do barriers exist that discourage active participation?

The potential for political participation

As this study has demonstrated, evidence exists that the Hispanic elderly do have the potential to become active participants at all levels of politics and policy and to become leaders. Some have been involved at a younger age, while many others show strong support for age related and Hispanic related politics. The major barriers to participation shown in this study are a lack of communication between the elderly and other Hispanics and generational conflicts. Assuming these barriers are overcome, the elderly would be active participants. In order, however, for Hispanic elderly to be likely participants in age related activities, they must show that they are becoming interested in age related issues.

Traditionally, however, Hispanics have maintained extended family structures (Maldonado, 1975; Miranda, 1975) and live in age integrated environments whereby they are not segregated by age (Leonard, 1967; Sotomayor, 1975). Age-related concepts such as retirement and leisure have been alien to older Hispanics (Moore, 1971; Dieppa, 1977). The fact that nursing home facilities are underutilized by Mexican American elderly (Eribes and Rawls, 1978) and that they prefer not to use them (Luevano, 1981) is further indication that they are not naturally prone to participate in strictly senior citizen activities.

Thus, to the extent that those traditional perceptions exist, it can be expected that Hispanic elders would not naturally gravitate toward exclusive age-related activities such as senior citizen centers.

Those traditional patterns, however, appear to be changing in some geographical areas, and the Hispanic elderly in those areas are less likely to perform traditional roles in the family (see chapter 1). Therefore, there exists a developing gap that must be filled. In a study of senior citizen clubs in the East Los Angeles "barrio," Cuellar (1978) found that elderly Chicanos created Hispanic senior clubs as a new social setting to redevelop interpersonal relationships. Furthermore, he found that these social clubs exist as a means for members to learn new social roles and relationships as elderly persons and thus fill a psychological and social void left when traditional roles, values and expectations associated with aging cease to exist in the urban, non-traditional setting. Other forms of voluntary associations Hispanics participate in as older persons include the Guadalupanas, (women's community service organization) and Sociedad Mutualistas (Mutual Aid Society). These organizations are long standing groups formed to assist barrio dwellers but are inordinately composed of elders (Valle, 1981).

To the extent that voluntary associations and senior citizen clubs encourage older persons to become politically active and serve as an organizing forum, it can be expected that Hispanic senior citizen clubs may lead some to greater involvement. Trela notes that although senior centers generally advance social and recreational goals, these groups may have far reaching political consequences (1971). He found that to the degree that Hispanic elders join senior centers, they may adopt age as a reference point from which social and political activities will build upon age related issues. That represents an important hypothesis concerning their political potential: as Hispanic elders participate in senior citizen clubs, they will be more likely to engage in age related social and political activities.

Two additional factors may also affect the political potential of older Hispanics to engage in age-related activities. Researchers in Hispanic gerontology have found that Mexican-American elderly perceive the onset of old age as occurring earlier than do Anglos (Bengtson, et al., 1977). Crouch (1972) found in West Texas, that two thirds of Hispanics felt that old age begins before sixty. That finding was verified in an East Los Angeles study (Cueller, 1978). Thus, as Hispanic professionals and advocates educate older Hispanics to the importance of age related activities and to the necessity of improving their social and economic positions, the perception of old age at an earlier age will be a driving force toward cognizance of themselves as senior citizens. In addition, when income and education are controlled, older persons will become more active than other age groups. Although a large proportion of Hispanic elderly are poor and have low levels of education rates, those factors in themselves do not mean that Hispanics are disproportionately inactive. Part of the reason for inactivity is due to income and education factors, and if and when they are improved, their propensity to be active may improve as well.

Therefore, the involvement of Hispanic seniors in age related voluntary activities, perceptions that they age at an earlier age and the finding that education and income, when controlled, do not inhibit involvement provide additional evidence that despite traditional values of age integrated and extended family activities, Hispanic elderly will become active in age related issues. Translating that interest into the political realm becomes the next logical step.

The 1981 White House Conference on Aging gave striking proof that Hispanic elders finally may be organizing around age related issues and may be pursuing political strategies to improve their position. Unlike the 1971 White House Conference on Aging, the 1981 conference planned to include minority elderly in proportion to their numbers in the population. That was an incentive for minority and Hispanic elderly and their advocates to become involved in the community forums and state and regional conferences that led to the national conference. In Los Angeles County, for example, out of the elected positions available for delegates to the national conference, at least half were filled by Hispanic older persons, which represented more than their proportional numbers. The Hispanic seniors accomplished that elective victory by organizing the Hispanic senior clubs and establishing a slate and voting as a block. That event was striking proof that under the proper circumstances, older Hispanics have the interest and ability to be involved politically.

Impact of Participation

If the older Hispanic becomes politically active,

157

what will be the impact and the consequences of those actions? Will it create changes in traditional social and familial relationships, age based politics and social policy, and Hispanic politics?

Social and familial relations

The impact on the traditional role of the family, church and neighborhood, vis a vis the Hispanic elderly, must be addressed in discussing the potential for political participation among older Hispanics. "Ageism" (discrimination by age) and accompanying age segregation of the elderly is a new phenomenon to the current cohort of Hispanic elders. The elderly face stereotypes and discrimination reflecting deep divisions by age in United States society. Will increased involvement in age related activities promote ageism and age segregation among Hispanics? Some researchers claim that the expansion of special policies and programs for the elderly segregate and stigmitize older persons despite the sincere motives of advocates to improve their well being (Estes, 1979). If that is true, it may contribute to a developing generation gap among many Hispanic families, particularly the upwardly mobile, urban families. With greater emphasis on age related activities and politics, older Hispanics may become less interested in the traditional roles of religious advocates and teachers, child rearers and participants in family decision-making -- roles pointed to as models for those emulating the uniqueness of Hispanic family ties. Instead they may become more interested in their peer and group activities, emphasizing commonality of age, group affiliation and social and political priorities. However, it may be that this generation gap has already occurred, irrespective of any renewed emphasis on political activities based on age, and therefore, this new orientation is simply filling a gap. In either event, it is safe to assume that increased involvement by elderly Hispanics in social groups, voluntary associations and political activities associated with being a senior citizen will affect traditional family and social roles. To those who point to Hispanic culture as an advantage in what they perceive to be an impersonal, technological, fast paced society, involvement may not be welcomed. To those who see change as inevitable andforesee increased assimilation among Hispanics of all age groups, increased political participation in age related activities may be a natural, healthy and beneficial trend for older

Hispanics.

Aged based politics and social policy

Increased political participation by Hispanic elders to better their conditions hinges on the assumption that they will become involved in political activities of older persons. However, organizations and groups advocating for older persons are primarily White, middle-class, English speaking organizations. They have not, and still do not, include substantial numbers of non-White, non-English speaking, poor older persons (e.g., Hispanics, Asians, Blacks). For that reason, the Asociacion Nacional Pro Personas Mayores and the National Hispanic Council on Aging were formed to promote Hispanic interests in gerontology. But as noted previously, those organizations have remained professional, middle-aged groups of individuals who may be Hispanic but may not necessarily relate to grass roots, community based groups of Hispanic seniors. Therefore, a challenge is presented to non-Hispanic aging groups, as well as to Hispanic organizations, to open their doors to the Hispanic senior citizen -- in terms of both membership and active participation. That it will occur in the near future remains doubtful. The constant quest by professionals for research and training opportunities, employment, status and salary advancements within the professions of gerontology and geriatrics will remain important priorities that may not necessarily coincide with the needs of older Hispanics for transportation, housing, health and income assistance, as well as the social and political benefits of being organized. At present, some professionals in gerontology attempt to organize Hispanic seniors on a community level and to advance their professional interests; but these remain objectives difficult to reconcile. Therefore, it becomes necessary for the Hispanic senior leadership, which exists in every community, to either form their own mass membership organizations composed of Hispanic elders and led by Hispanic elders or to join mass membership organizations such as the American Association of Retired Persons/National Retired Teachers Association (AARP/NRTA) and the Gray Panthers, who already work closely with community groups, albeit composed of English speaking senior citizens. How that occurs is uncertain and will depend upon effective organizing strategies and tactics. Should it be successful, however, it may lead to further polarization between professionals and senior citizens;

with the Hispanic elders active in groups that promote their age related interests and Hispanic professionals active in professional and academic organizations. That may create tension and social distance but it also may create opportunities to advance Hispanic gerontology from different approaches.

The development of mass membership organizations composed primarily of Hispanic seniors will contribute to an expansion of senior power among Hispanics, particularly as their numbers increase. As shown earlier, Hispanic elders have higher rates of voting than other age segments of the Hispanic population, although it is relatively low, compared to White and Black elderly. Nonetheless, it will have significant implications for the development of social policies benefiting Hispanic elders.

Aged based organizations are considered by several writers as important in affecting social and public policy. The Townsend movement of the 1930s (Holtzman, 1963) and the McClain organization in California (Pinner et al.,1959) were early aged based movements engaged in political activities, primarily pension reform. Contemporary aged based organizations engaged in political activities include the National Council on Senior Citizens, founded in the early 1960s to work for the passage of Medicare (NCSC); the National Black Caucus, an advocacy coalition of Black professionals; the National Indian Council on Aging, organized to represent Native American elderly; and the National Hispanic Council on Aging. These organizations are examples of aged based organizations that attempt to influence social policy through lobbying, confrontation politics and other means.

Writers concerned with the politics of aging have debated the extent of political influence of aged based organizations. Cottrell (1971:35) sees groups such as the National Council of Senior Citizens and the American Association of Retired Persons as having "a great deal of political clout." The Association of Old Age and Invalidity Pensioner in Denmark is considered by Friis (1969:144) to be an influential pressure group. Donahue and Tibbits (1962) allude to the political power of aging groups, power derived through the direct participation of older persons in the electorate process and in the activities of organizations. Binstock (1972, 1974), Hudson and Binstock (1976) and Pratt (1976), however, are somewhat cynical about the power of aged based organizations. Hudson and Binstock state that "neither the goals that these organizations seek, nor the power they have for attempting to implement them seem likely to engender a marked reordering of political process or public priorities" (Hudson & Binstock, 1976:386). Essentially, they argue that the term "political power" is vague, which makes it difficult to gauge accurately the political power of aged based organizations. They state that the amount of political power possessed by aged based organizations lies between two extremes of the power continuum: "the extreme of controlling power and the extreme of powerlessness."

In general, regardless of any assessment of aging based organizations' power, these organizations clearly can affect social policy. Hudson and Binstock observe that aged based organizations are "very active and skilled in gaining access to elected and appointed public officials, to career bureaucrats and legislative staffs and to political parties and other politically active organizations in Washington" (Hudson & Binstock, 1976:385). In a sense, the issue of these organizations' political power, when seen in the context of the political situation of older Hispanics, is a relative issue. Contemporary aged-based organizations illuminate the political powerlessness of elderly Hispanics. Except for the Asociacion and the National Hispanic Council on Aging, no national aged based organizations speak for the Spanish speaking elderly.

Therefore, in order for Hispanic elders to influence social policy issues, it will be imperative that they do one of the following: develop links with Hispanic organizations and leaders, develop links with established aged-based organizations that are primarily white, or develop their own national and politically influential senior citizen organizations.

These options are not mutually exclusive; elderly Hispanics can do all three. Presently, it appears that Hispanic elders, to the extent they are involved, are attempting to develop community based clubs and organizations. For example, in many communities Hispanic elders are succeeding in using their community activism to win seats on advisory commissions and committees that represent elders on a local level. In addition, some work closely with church and neighborhood organizations. In order to influence

161

policy -- be it city, county, state or national -- more
organizing will be needed and it will take time.
Linking with Hispanic political leaders is an efficient
way to acquire political power in the short term. In
California the state legislature includes several
Hispanic assemblymen and state senators who advocate
for increased services to Hispanic seniors. However,
those politicians have competing demands and pressures
to assist many constituents, and their necessity for
political contributions and support influence to a
large degree the individuals and organizations that
will gain access to them. If Hispanic seniors lack the
ability to raise funds or demonstrate a strong voting
block they may not get consistent priority attention by
elected officials. Therefore, one possible avenue to
political power may be to link up with established
aging organizations such as the National Council on
Aging, American Association for Retired
Persons/National Retired Teachers Association and Gray
Panthers and utilize their considerable clout. That
has not yet occurred; but it warrants increased
exploration as a possible method. The last method
mentioned, developing their own aged based
organizations, has begun. Again, they have yet to
demonstrate sufficient influence to leverage priority
attention by elected officials.

Assuming that in time Hispanic elders acquire
political leverage to influence policy, what specific
areas may be emphasized? Current areas of social
policy concerns for older persons include the solvency
of Social Security and Medicare, the impact of
inflation on fixed incomes, the high cost of housing,
age discrimination, crime against the elderly and
increased work opportunities for older persons.
Elderly Hispanics can be expected to be concerned with
these issues. They will also be concerned with other
social policy issues reflecting their cultural and
historical position in this society. For example, the
preservation of the family and related values of a
basically agrarian, conservative environment; the
development of bilingual and bicultural programs; and
relationships with Mexico, Puerto Rico and Cuba (where
many retain contacts with family and friends) may be as
important as the issues that affect all older persons.
However, they may not be congruent with the priorities
of established aged based organizations and Hispanic
leaders. Examples abound. Efforts by the California
state legislature to pass legislation targeting social
services to the elderly with cultural and linguistic

difficulties; development of nursing homes staffed with Spanish speaking personnel and located in Hispanic neighborhoods; use of folk medicine in hospice settings; and traveling to border areas of Mexico to obtain medical care have created disagreements with established aging organizations who feel that social services should be universal and not targeted to a specific ethnic group. These efforts indicate that as Hispanic elderly acquire the necessary power and sophistication to influence social policies, it may not always create unity with non-Hispanic elderly. Yet, in spite of potential differences in policy directions, objectives by established aging organizations are not totally different from the needs of Hispanic elders. They all face the need for income security, health care, housing and transportation. Therefore, broad areas of common concern exist that make it possible for Hispanic elders and other seniors to work together.

Hispanic politics

At a time when Hispanics in general are acquiring political power in various regions of the country, the fact remains that Hispanic elders have not been considered a constituency sufficiently important to be courted by political leaders. To a large extent, that is due to the traditional belief that the elders are part of an age integrated familial setting; thus, if the entire family is involved, Hispanic elders automatically will be included. It is also due to ignorance about the changing demographic trends in the Hispanic population that are resulting in larger numbers of Hispanics sixty years and over and in their growing interest in age-specific activities. To the extent that Hispanic elders are increasing in numbers and becoming active in senior citizen activities, it may benefit Hispanic political leaders to understand their needs and concerns -- if for no other reason than to seek support from an important political constituency.

Therefore, increased involvement of Hispanic elders in aged based organizations, whether Hispanic oriented or part of larger established aged based organizations, may pressure Hispanic politicians to focus on aging issues such as senior citizen centers, nutrition programs, social security, geriatrics and long term care and the need for bilingual, bicultural programs for Hispanic seniors. That Hispanic politicians are recognizing this need is apparent in

163

many areas, including Los Angeles, San Antonio, New York and Puerto Rico. However, another issue remains: will Hispanic elders play a leadership role in Hispanic politics? As indicated in this study, many Hispanic elders perceive themselves to be excluded from positions of leadership and find lack of communication with Hispanic activists a major problem.

That may result in two parallel developments: a rise in Hispanic power reflected in Hispanic political organizations and groups and a rise in Hispanic senior power reflected in their own political organizations. That parallel development will mean tension and competition for leadership and visibility but may not be altogether negative. Hispanic seniors may be in a more influential position if they develop themselves as a separate political constituency with adequate power to leverage concessions and agreements with Hispanic leaders and organizations. If White senior citizen groups have felt a need to develop separate political organizations apart from general political groups, there is little reason to believe that Hispanics will not also find it a preferred method. Inevitably, astute Hispanic politicians will recognize the higher levels of political interest and voting among Hispanic elders and will court them. Whether that develops into substantive gains for Hispanic elders may depend in large part on their own political clout to ensure a follow through of political promises.

Additional implications of political involvement by Hispanic elders may focus on added incentives for culturally relevant services. Hispanic seniors remain closest to traditional values and cultures -- more so than younger segments of the population. If they acquire political leverage, it can be assumed that they will provide added pressure for services in Spanish and for programs that are culturally based. To the extent that bilingualism remains a political issue for Hispanic politicians, the Hispanic elder is an important political base for support.

Future Directions

This study has demonstrated the barriers that confront Hispanic elders in political participation as well as the potential for becoming active. The implications for increased participation also have been discussed. Up to this point, the discussion has focused on today's cohorts of elderly. The future of

the politics of Hispanic aging will depend, in large
measure, on changes occurring in future cohorts of
older persons. Cutler (1981) identifies and discusses
political characteristics of elderly cohorts of the
early decades of the next century. He predicts several
changes occurring: increased educational attainment,
which will increase participation in voluntary
associations and sophistication in political issues;
erosion of partisanship and lessened attachment to
political parties, issues and candidates; and an
increase in politically relevant age consciousness.
These factors may lead to even greater political power
for senior citizens in this country. Whether Hispanic
cohorts will witness similar trends is uncertain.
Discussions on the subject are based largely on
speculation. As is generally the case, Cutler's
research has not focused on subgroups of the elderly
population, and thus it is difficult to generalize to
Hispanics. However, several educated guesses can be
made about future changes in Hispanic cohorts. Several
may be similar to Cutler's: they will be better
educated, healthier and have higher incomes. These
factors may lead to increased leisure time and the
ability to become involved in organizations and
political activities, with greater attention to age
related activities. Political sophistication will
increase, in large part because future cohorts will
become better versed in English, socialized to a
participant political culture and politically
acculturated. Should these scenarios unfold, then
clearly the future Hispanic elder will have greater
influence on politics and policy and will move from a
politics of deference to a politics of competition.
But will current preoccupations with social policy
issues remain the same? Perhaps not. If observations
of middle-aged Hispanics are correct, we are witnessing
an age cohort that was affected by events such as the
depression, World War II and the discrimination
characteristic of that period. This is a population
that, in general, strived mightily to assimilate with
many attempting to diminish their ethnic identity. It
may well be that current attention to linguistic and
culturally relevant services and traditions may not be
as important to them as other priorities, perhaps those
more in line with the general elderly population.
Those changes, should they occur, will have
significance to the current preoccupations of Hispanic
gerontologists and advocates who stress programs and
services that reflect culture and language and that in
turn result in separate services for Hispanic elders.

There are, of course, mitigating circumstances that may affect these changes. The follow-up cohort, those now thirty to forty, have been more in tune with Hispanic culture (as reflected in the various Hispanic cultural movements of the 1960s and 1970s), which may counteract assimilation tendencies of this upcoming generation of Hispanic elders. In addition, the vast immigration occurring from Mexico, Central and South America, Puerto Rico and Cuba will guarantee a large population of Hispanics who are non-English speaking, non-assimiliated and non-acculturated and who will in all likelihood practice a politics of deference.

Those groups will insure pressure for changes similar to those of today's Hispanic elderly. The extent to which these competing forces will balance out is impossible to estimate. But it is certain that future cohorts will undergo changes that in turn will affect political directions and policy choices.

Conclusion

In conclusion, this study has demonstrated that the Hispanic elderly are not active participants in the political process, relative to other elderly groups. However, the barriers preventing that can be overcome with better communication, increased income and education, and effective outreach by Hispanics and established aging organizations. The potential for Hispanic elderly to become actively engaged in Hispanic politics and senior citizen activities exists. Should it occur, it can have influence on social policies for the elderly, cultural nationalism and politics in general. How that ultimately plays out remains uncertain. This study is only one of a few that have explored the political behavior of older Hispanics. Many questions remain unanswered. For example:

1) What are the organizing strategies for bringing together Hispanic seniors?

2) Should Hispanic seniors develop age related groups, and if so, is there a risk that ageism will occur?

3) What are the changes occurring in traditional Hispanic values that affect the role of older persons in the family and their community, and how will that affect their political behavior?

4) What intergenerational issues will arise between the young, middle-aged and elderly segments of the Hispanic population if older Hispanics organize politically?

5) What are the variations between subgroups of Hispanic elderly--Puerto Ricans, Cubans, Latin Americans and Mexican Americans?

6) What personality traits (e.g., motivation, efficacy) are most important in encouraging participation by Hispanic elderly?

7) How does the rise of aged based organizations for Hispanics relate to the rise of aged based organizations for the elderly in general?

8) What should be the mix of social service programs to meet the needs of Hispanic elderly, and to what extent should cultural and linguistic elements be incorporated in those services?

Those and many other questions remain to be addressed in future studies of the politics of Hispanic aging. It will be important to obtain more data and information as well as develop a theoretical base for understanding this knowledge. Much of what is learned will apply to other ethnic groups, but much will be unique to Hispanics because of their historical, cultural and political position in this country. That Hispanic elders will play an increasingly significant role in this country and in their ethnic groups is certain. The extent to which they are allowed to participate is uncertain. Hopefully, scholars, politicians and private citizens will examine this area closely and contribute to the political involvement of elder Hispanics. It is further hoped that as Hispanics and the White elderly increase their political activism that a partnership will be reached with Hispanic elders.

APPENDIX A

RESEARCH DESIGN

This section seeks to describe the methodology used to generate empirical evidence to answer several interrelated questions:

1. What is the political participation of the elderly compared to the White elderly and the Hispanics in general?

2. What are the older Hispanics' attitudes toward Hispanic politics and senior citizen activities?

3. Are generational conflicts and ideological disagreements viewed by older Hispanics as major factors in nonparticipation by the Hispanic aged in Hispanic related politics?

4. What personal experiences have the older Hispanics undergone which may have influenced their political attitudes?

5. What is the older Hispanics' extent of participation in activities related to age?

Study Design

The research design entails selection of a random sample of elderly Hispanics, measurement of their political attitudes and rates of political activities, and examination of their attitudes about Hispanic politics and senior activities. A random survey of 106 older Hispanics was conducted in areas of San Jose, California, containing high numbers of older Mexican-Americans with low incomes. Data collected in the survey include rate of political activity, political attitudes, and descriptive information about personal experiences. Specifically the objective is to describe the relationships between the independent variables (socioeconomic status, generational relations, ethnicity, political socialization, attitudes) and the dependent variables (political participation, political attitudes). This relationship should provide profiles of the older Hispanics' political behavior and determine which variables are significantly related to the politically active and

169

politically inactive respondents. The analysis consists of frequencies, cross-tabulation, correlations, and content analysis of the unstructured segment of the interview.

Hypotheses

1. That because of their social, cultural, and political position, the elderly Hispanics will be found to cluster near the low end of the hierarchy of political involvement (apathetic, least active).

2. That those who rank low in a sense of political efficacy and citizen duty will be politically alienated and will show such alienation through low rates of political participation.

3. That those with negative experiences in politics during their lifetimes will express negative feelings about participation in politics.

4. That because of discouragement (generational conflicts) by younger Hispanics, the level of participation in Hispanic politics for older Hispanics will be low.

5. That because of ideological disagreement with the Hispanic political movement, older Hispanics will express negative attitudes toward Hispanic politics.

Dependent Variables

The dependent variables, which are each multivariate, consist of social and political indicators of participation. The primary dependent variable is political participation. The six separate variables describing this primary dependent variable concern six dimensions of political and social participation. As a guide to the discusion of dimensions which constitute the dependent variables, refer to the outline below.

Dimensions of Political and Social Participation

I. Political Participation

170

A. Political Awareness

    1. Familiarity of leaders and organizations
    2. Support of leaders and organizations
    3. Discussion of politics and public problems

B. Membership in Formal Organizations

    1. Membership in unions
    2. Membership in political groups
    3. Membership in civic groups

C. Voting Behavior

    1. Registration to vote
    2. Total vote frequency

D. Past Political Activities

    1. Chicano related politics
    2. Old-age related politics
    3. General citizenship

II. Social Participation

A. Religious Activity

    1. Membership in church
    2. Membership in religious organizations

B. Senior Citizen Activity

    1. Membership in senior clubs

Political awareness

The degree of familiarity with and support of Hispanic leaders and organizations, as well as interest in political discussions, measures political awareness. Familiarity is measured by asking the respondents if they have heard of (or are familiar with) six political Hispanic leaders and organizations. Asking the respondent if he supports or agrees with the activities of these leaders and organizations determines support. Discussion of politics is one of the least active of political activities. Nonetheless, it indicates a person's interest in politics, even though he may not be actively involved. This variable is measured by asking the respondent if he discusses politics with the family, friends, neighbors, priest, community leaders, government bureaucrats, or public officials.

Membership in formal organizations

Among the dependent variables measuring political participation, this is the most active referent for political activities among the dimensions of political participation, since participation by older Hispanics will probably require substantial energy and commitment because of their low socioeconomic status and age. Three variables measure membership in formal organizations: (1) membership in unions, (2) membership in civic groups such as women's clubs and Model Cities advisory boards, and (3) membership in political organizations such as GI Forum and La Raza Unida Party.

Voting behavior

Voting is one of the most frequently used measures of political participation, particularly in the politics of age (Riley and Foner, 1968). This study examines voting frequency in local, state, and national elections. On the basis of voting frequency in three types of elections an index measuring total vote frequency is also developed. Another referent used for this variable is whether the respondent is registered to vote.

Past political activities

As one of its many objectives, this study assesses the type of politics the older persons engaged in during adult years. For this purpose Milbrath's hierarchy of political involvement is used. Milbrath (1965) developed a hierarchy of political involvement which divides political activities by three categories: spectator, transitional, and gladiatorial. Spectator activities characterize those who may be termed leisure-time respondents. They expend a minimum of effort without great personal commitment. Persons involved in transitional activities are those who are likely to be making the first steps toward activities in the gladiatorial category. The activities can be either the first steps in becoming gladiators or an extreme step in the spectator

172

category. Gladiatorial activities are characterized by a greater expenditure of energy and greater personal commitment than those in the spectator or transitional categories. The hierarchy includes most common political activities "that characterize the normal processes of a democracy" (Milbrath, 1965:18). The hierarchy assumes that political participation is cumulative; persons who engage in one political action often engage in others as well. Milbrath's hierarchy of political involvement is given below, with those most often engaged being listed at the bottom and those least often engaged being listed at the top.

Hierarchy of Political Involvement

1. Gladiatorial Activities
    a. Holding public and party office
    b. Being a candidate for office
    c. Protesting and demonstrating
    d. Soliciting political funds
    e. Attending a caucus or a strategy meeting
    f. Becoming an active member in a political party
    g. Contributing time in a political campaign

2. Transitional Activities
    a. Attending a political meeting or rally
    b. Making a monetary contribution to a party or candidate
    c. Contacting a public official or political leader

3. Spectator
    a. Wearing a button or putting a sticker on the car
    b. Attempting to talk another into voting a certain way
    c. Initiating a political discussion
    d. Voting
    e. Exposing oneself to political stimuli

4. Apathetics
    a. No political activity

For this study Milbrath's hierarchy is further subdivided into three types of politics: Hispanic related, old-age related, and general citizenship. These categories classify the types of political activities the older person may have engaged in. The three classifications are defined as follows:

173

1. Hispanic related: Activities directly associated with Hispanic cultural and political actions (for example, picketing for the Farmworkers Union, lobbying for the Community Service Organization, being an active member of the GI Forum, and attending city council meetings in support of Hispanic issues).

2. Age-related: Activities primarily concerned with the specific interests of the elderly (for example, lobbying in the state capitol for pensions, organizing old-age groups, picketing the city council for reduced bus fares, and recruiting members for Hispanic senior citizen clubs).

3. General citizenship: Activities not specifically related to the above (for example, voting in local, state, and general elections; campaigning for candidates without special concern for candidates' views on Hispanic or senior citizen issues; and writing letters to congressmen).

The hierarchy is not intended to reveal accurate frequencies of activities; instead it provides a general picture of past political participation.

Religious activity

Religiousness has been mentioned in studies of minority elderly as an important factor in the lives of older persons. Sotomayor (1973) found that the church and its socioreligious clubs are the sole recreation and source of social interaction among older Hispanics. Rubenstein (1972) described the church as the major formal social organization for most Black people. To older Blacks it is a religious organization, a social order, and an educational and welfare agency which provides leadership in community issues. Gallo (1974) cited the religious factor as predicating political preferences. He stated that religion can significantly determine ideological orientation in local politics. He found that strict Catholics, primarily among the immigrants and first-generation respondents, tended to take conservative positions; marginal Catholics, especially of the third generation, tended to take liberal positions; while moderate Catholics tended to follow centrist politics in local politics (Gallo, 1974:134).

In the expectation that participation in the church and in religious activities would serve an important social, recreational, and perhaps political function in the Hispanic barrio, two variables were chosen to assess the degree of religious activity. The variables measure attendance at church and membership in religious organizations. Religious activity also serves as an independent variable. To determine the effect of religious activity on political participation--attendance at church, membership in religious organizations, and an additional variable are measured against political participation. The additional variable--whether the priest talks about politics in church--is intended to assess the impact of a priest's political discussion on the attitudes of older Hispanics toward politics.

Senior citizen activity

In assessing factors related to possible political activity among older Hispanics, one must examine the extent of their involvement in senior citizen activities. Recently social gerontologists have paid particular attention to the role and function of age based voluntary associations. This interest has been encouraged by findings that suggest a relationship between involvement in senior citizen organizations and certain forms of political participation, the degrees of political involvement, and the desire for social change, as well as the development of age consciousness and feelings of political efficacy (Olsen, 1972; Trela, 1972, 1973). For example, in a study of senior citizen centers and other old-age group memberships, Trela found that these groups provide a context for political change and heightened political consciousness (Trela, 1971:118-23). Therefore, to the extent that the older Hispanics participates in senior centers and age related activities, one may expect that his political awareness and political participation will increase.

This study, however, expects that the older Hispanic will be alienated from senior citizen activities. Traditionally, most Hispanic social activities have been age heterogeneous, and this has allowed for a commonality of interests among all age groups in the Hispanic population. In contrast, senior citizen activities are age homogeneous. Thus, the study anticipates that the older Hispanic will not have acquired an "aging group consciousness" (Rose, 1968). Whether the older Hispanic is conscious of the need to

175

organize and participate around age related issues is uncertain. Lacking further documentation, this study will assume that the older Hispanic is not age-group conscious.

Independent Variables

Like the dependent variables, the independent variables are multivariate, consisting of attitudes, correlates, and factors which affect political participation. In contrast to the dependent variables, the independent variables are more complex. These independent variables include:

1. Political efficacy and sense of citizen duty
2. Political socialization (historical development)
3. Ethnic identification
4. Generational conflicts and ideological disagreements
5. Socioeconomic status and functional ability
6. Attitudes

Political efficacy and sense of citizen duty

The senses of political efficacy and citizen duty are personality traits which relate to political participation. Individuals with a sense of political efficacy and citizen duty are more likely to participate. The scales of political efficacy and citizen duty consist of four and five items, respectively, and measure the levels of feelings of efficacy and citizen duty among the respondents (Robinson et al., 1968). Although these two scales have been widely used, they have not previously been used on a sample of minority aged. Since these scales needed to be translated into Spanish, difficulties had been anticipated and borne out during the interviews. The scales were cumbersome and accounted for a number of respondents who did not answer specific items on the scales. Nevertheless, the scales are considered a useful measure of sense of efficacy and citizen duty among those who responded to the scale items.

Political socialization (historical developments)

For this study political socialization is considered to be the sum total of childhood and adult experiences which have a bearing on political behavior. Political socialization is operationalized through a

176

series of questions which measure the amount of
political stimuli in the home during childhood. These
questions include parental involvement in politics and
a discussion of politics in the home. It was
anticipated that the recall ability of the respondents
would limit their responses to these questions.
Therefore the researcher employed an open-ended
question which assessed the personal experiences in the
respondents' lives that affected their attitudes toward
politics. Political socialization thus includes
whatever historical or personal incidents affect the
respondents' political attitudes and political
participation.

Ethnic identification

Ethnic identification is considered, for this
study, to be a measure of the relationship to a
political structure. For example, if a respondent
identifies closely with Mexico and was born and raised
there, he will probably be more likely to possess
political orientations characteristic of a Mexican
political culture than if he had been born and raised
in the United States. This is a limited measure of
ethnic identification and acculturation. By
determining the significance between low political
participation and strong ethnic identification, Chapter
IV, "Characteristics of the Politically Active and
Politically Inactive," examines the validity of
associating these variables with political behavior.
Ethnic identification is measured by the following
variables: birthplace, country raised in, recentness
of immigration, frequency of visits to Mexico, and
citizenship.

Generational conflicts and ideological disagreements

Chapter II presented generational conflicts and
ideological disagreements as factors affecting the
political behavior of older Hispanics. Generational
conflicts with younger Hispanics and ideological
disagreements with Hispanic politics would probably
lead to negative attitudes toward Hispanic politics and
inactivity in Hispanic politics. These factors can
appear in attitudes which include feelings of
disrespect for Hispanics, feelings that Hispanics do
not understand the older person, dislike of the
Hispanic political movement, and feelings of distrust
for Hispanic activists.

Attitudes

One of the central premises of the study is that respondents' attitudes will illuminate factors which may account for the variation in political participation. These attitudes can include a variety of feelings and perceptions about the reasons that older persons are not active in Hispanic politics, senior activities, and general citizenship. Possible attitudes could include apathy, fear, poor self-image, and negative role expectations. Those apathetic may be uninterested in political activities. Those fearful may be afraid of discrimination, exploitation, or deprivation such as loss of citizenship. Those with poor self-image may feel useless and too old to participate. Those with negative role expectations may act out traditional roles, which do not encourage participation. For example, a female may feel that she must stay at home to care for her family and husband and that she should not be involved in outside activities. An older person may feel that his church and religion are the answers to his problems rather than political involvement.

Socioeconomic status and functional ability

Socioeconomic status and functional ability were identified as relating to access to political participation. Socioeconomic status includes age, income, sex, occupation, and education. Functional ability consists of health and physical mobility.

Data Collection

The questionnaire

Primary data were collected in a structured questionnaire which was designed to yield information on the following areas.

1. Socioeconomic profile--age, income, occupation, education.
2. Political participation--type of activities, frequency of activities.
3. Awareness index--knowledge of political issues, leaders, and organizations.
4. Indices of political efficacy and citizen duty.
5. Attitudes--projective tests, open-ended questions.

178

6. Political socialization--historical developments, personal experiences.

The questionnaire was prepared in two stages: a
pretested version and a revised version. An initial
survey instrument was designed for pretesting. Five
Puerto Rican elderly in Boston and five Hispanic older
persons in San Jose took part in the pretesting. The
revised instrument was then administered to 106
individuals in the sample of older Hispanics.

The first section of the revised questionnaire
consisted primarily of closed-ended questions about
socioeconomic status and family structure. The second
section sought to examine the dependent variable of
political awareness, membership in formal
organizations, voting, and past and current political
activities. This section was fairly structured and
consisted of closed-ended questions. The third section
sought to assess the sense of political efficacy and
citizen duty. The fourth section included a series of
items intended to elicit respondents' attitudes about
senior activities, Hispanic politics, and
intergenerational relations. Most questions were
open-ended and offered the respondents an opportunity
to voice their feelings and opinions. The final
section dealt with the content area of political
socialization and historical developments. It
consisted of a series of structured questions which
measured childhood socialization and employed one
open-ended question, which allowed the respondents to
discuss those incidents which influenced their
attitudes and political participation.

Interviews

In conducting successful personal interviews with
older Hispanics, a questioner must contend with several
factors. These include the casting of proposed
questions, language regionality, the interpersonal
relation, and community support. The survey group was
unique and had to be approached in a manner that would
neither offend nor threaten. This researcher's
approach is described in hopes that it will benefit
other researchers endeavoring to interview older
Hispanics.

Casting of proposed questions

It was determined from the outset that the

179

research instrument would be cast in bilingual formats and in modes of address and terminology congruent with local language. The casting of proposed questions in Spanish was first seen as a critical starting point in the interview foundation process, particularly since some terms and phrases appropriate in English are inappropriate in Spanish and could easily skew the interview process. For example, the scales on political efficacy and citizen duty were difficult to translate into Spanish while retaining their intended meaning. Conducting the interview in English overcame this in part; when Spanish was necessary, the researcher translated carefully so that the meanings were clear. Nevertheless, the scales proved difficult to use in the actual interview, and language, in large part, accounted for the high number of respondents who did not complete both scales.

Language regionality

Language regionality presented an additional consideration in interview-format design. For example, unless specifically introduced by the respondents, the term "Chicano" was not used in the field. Most respondents disliked the term "Chicano" and preferred "Mexicano." To the older person the word "Chicano" still retains its literal translation ("a person of very low status"), while the contemporary definition ("a politically and culturally aware Mexican-American") has not yet been adopted by them. Another term preferred by the older persons was "La persona de mayor edad," which means "the elderly." Other words for "aged," such as "viejo," had to be chosen with care so as not to show disrespect for the older person.

The interpersonal factor: Platicado

Valle (1974) describes the interpersonal factor as the platicado mode of interaction among Hispanics. He asserts that unless the interviewer and respondent are sufficiently attracted to each other to permit a "pleasing sociable conversation," the interview will not take place. In achieving "mutual attractiveness" and "a pleasing sociable conversation," the interviewer must pass from the formal level of hablando (speaking to) and conversando (conversing) to the personal level of platicando (transacting); only then can the interviewer expect to elicit themes at the core of the interviewer's concern.

The _platicado_ mode of interaction especially
applies to older Hispanics. Throughout the survey the
interview generally could proceed smoothly only after
the interviewer indicated a personal interest in the
respondent and his environment--his home and objects
within the home, which symbolized the personality and
life of that particular respondent. Once the
respondent felt comfortable with the interviewer,
questions and answers progressed more easily.
Platicando generally resulted in some loss of
information since time was consumed achieving the
necessary rapport. Nevertheless, the rapport developed
between interviewer and respondent compensated for the
loss.

Community support

On a broader level, the interviewing required
support from the barrio communites and "sponsorship"
from those agencies and groups who provide services and
support to the older Hispanics. Support entails active
cooperation in finding and encouraging older Hispanics
to participate, and sponsorship is the ability to use
an organization's or individual's name as someone who
is aware of and in agreement with the study. The
residents of San Jose are politically aware and
recognize that researchers are not always good for the
community. As Torres-Gil (1972) documents, many
minority communities have been used by academicians and
researchers, yet have not received compensation from
those who have benefited from the poverty and culture
which provide substance for many research projects.
Since San Jose, in particular, has frequently been
studied, many of the residents have become wary of
academicians who appear with a satchelful of
questions. With this environment facing an
interviewer, he must obtain the support and sponsorship
of those groups and organizations which have legitimacy
in the community. Having come from the area and having
been involved in community issues, the researcher
acquired the needed support from the Hispanic senior
clubs, several individuals well known to older
Hispanics, and the sponsorship from the priests in the
east and west sides of San Jose. The study's purposes
were explained to these persons, and the potential
usefulness of this information was described. Their
invaluable assistance made the study possible.

Analysis

This phase of the study involved recasting and transferring the information collected into a form that a computer could handle. The data were submitted to a series of operations and tests which would enable statistical analysis. The operations included editing the questionnaires, coding, key-punching, and programming. The statistical tests included frequency distributions, correlations, and cross-tabulations. To reveal the variables appropriate for inclusion in this study, the data were analyzed through an examination of frequency distributions. The distribution also aided the collapsing of variables. Procedures were developed to construct indices which would measure aggregate political participation and attitudinal support for political issues, from particular independent and dependent variables. The relationships between the variables were examined with cross-tabulations (SPSS, Data-Text). The hypotheses were tested by the Pearson Chi-Square (X^2) test of association.

APPENDIX B

DATA COLLECTION INSTRUMENTS
AND PROCEDURES

Data Processing Procedures

As the questionnaires were received, each was examined for completeness and accuracy. After all interviews were completed a codebook was established on the model of the data-text system. A code book was necessitated since numerical values for responses were not placed on the questionnaire. Ideally, coding should be done on the questionnaire to reduce error. This was not considered feasible because of the large number of open-ended questions and a variety of unanticipated responses. There were no missing data. Each question utilized a "NA" (not applicable), "DK" (don't know), or "NR" (no reply). After the establishment of a codebook, the raw data were transferred directly onto IBM sheets. Since three persons assisted in the operation, the researcher randomly examined 50 percent of the questionnaires for accuracy. The IBM sheets were subsequently key-punched and verified at the Harvard Computer Center. Next, the raw data were tabulated and subjected to several statistical tests, including frequency distributions, correlations, and cross-tabulations. The data utilized Data-Text for frequencies and cross-tabulations, and utilized SPSS for correlations.

Survey Procedures

Ten census tracts were selected in the San Jose target area. These census tracts are: 5040, 5037.02, 5036.02, 5036.01, 5011, 5012, 5019, 5023, 5020, 5004. Approximately 10 respondents were selected from each census tract although three or four census tracts had from 10 to 15 respondents. The reason was that some census tracts had few older persons and these were difficult to locate. Therefore, in the interest of time, census tracts (which had been randomly selected) with unusually high numbers of older Hispanics were assigned more than 10 respondents to be interviewed. Figures on the number of Spanish-speaking elderly in each census tract were available in The Aging Population of Santa Clara County: A Study (1973).

183

Survey Area Neighborhoods

The survey area includes three major Hispanic barrios: East, West, and Park. The East and West sides are considered by the Hispanic community of San Jose as established concentrations of Hispanics; that is, they have existed for many years and have a sense of community. The East side is roughly situated geographically between the Bayshore Freeway (Highway 101) and the foothills of the Diablo Range. The West Side roughly covers the area between the downtown district and the city of Willow Glen. The Park area is not an established or recognized neighborhood. It is a mixture of White and Hispanic families located between the Bayshore Freeway and the downtown area. The name "Park" was given by the researcher because no name had previously been assigned to this barrio.

The Survey

Pretesting

Pretesting consisted of interviewing five Puerto Rican older persons in the South end of Boston (a housing project) and five Mexican-American older persons in San Jose (primarily from the Libertad Center). The pretesting revealed that the original questionnaire needed revision. For example, some questions were misleading and had to be rewritten. The form of primary introduction had to be changed from a somewhat formal businesslike approach to a more informal personal approach (the platicado mode). The original questionnaire was too long; it took approximately one and one-half to two hours to complete. The revised questionnaire took approximately 45 minutes without the final open-ended question. The open-ended question dealing with the personal experiences of the respondents added from a half hour to two hours, depending on the respondents' willingness to be interviewed.

Resource persons

The researcher was fortunate in acquiring the sponsorship of two priests, one in the East side and the other in the West side, who knew many older persons. In addition, the director of the Libertad Club and various individuals actively involved with older persons cooperated with the researcher. They informed various persons of my potential visits and the purpose of the study. They personally introduced the researcher to key contacts among the elderly. Therefore the refusal rate was much lower than anticipated. Since no listing was obtained which listed older persons by name, age, and address, mailmen became key figures in locating the respondents.

APPENDIX C

SUPPLEMENTARY DATA

The following eight tables provide detailed frequencies and percentages on familiarity with and support of leaders and organizations, membership in organizations and church groups, voting rate, and the activities in the hierarchy of political involvement. Reference is made to these tables throughout Chapters III and IV.

TABLE C-1

RESPONDENTS' FAMILIARITY WITH LEADERS AND ORGANIZATIONS

Leaders and Organizations	Number	Never Heard Of		Heard of		Familiar With	
		N	%	N	%	N	%
GI Forum	105	59	56	35	33	11	10
MAPA	104	71	68	27	26	6	6
La Raza Unida	106	69	65	26	25	11	10
UFW	105	23	22	32	30	50	48
Libertad Center	100	37	37	40	40	23	23
La Confederacion	101	72	71	20	20	9	9
Gonzalez	98	74	76	18	18	6	6
Chavez	102	21	21	14	14	67	66
Gutierrez	97	79	81	11	11	7	7
Garza	96	46	48	26	27	24	25
Abeytia	96	48	50	25	26	23	24
Sarinana	101	42	42	29	29	30	30

TABLE C-2

RESPONDENTS' SUPPORT OF LEADERS AND ORGANIZATIONS

Leaders and Organizations	Number	Support		Do Not Support	
		N	%	N	%
GI Forum	28	24	86	4	14
MAPA	20	17	85	3	15
La Raza Unida	28	15	54	13	46
UFW	61	55	90	6	10
Libertad Center	45	40	89	5	11
La Confederacion	17	14	82	3	18
Gonzalez	19	12	63	7	37
Chavez	61	53	87	8	13
Gutierrez	12	8	67	4	33
Garza	37	34	92	3	8
Abeytia	33	16	48	17	52
Sarinana	38	35	92	3	8

TABLE C-3
RESPONDENTS' MEMBERSHIP IN ORGANIZATIONS

Organization	Number	Not a Member		Attend Regularly		Attend Infrequently		Never Attend	
		N	%	N	%	N	%	N	%
Union	104	98	94	0	0	5	5	1	1
Civic	103	97	94	3	3	3	3	0	0
Political	103	93	90	5	5	5	5	0	0
Libertad	104	96	92	5	5	3	3	0	0
Alma	103	99	96	2	2	2	2	0	0
Gardner	103	99	96	2	2	2	2	0	0

TABLE C-4
RESPONDENTS' VOTING FREQUENCY

Election	Number	Regularly		Occasionally		Seldom		Never	
		N	%	N	%	N	%	N	%
National	63	23	37	10	16	6	10	24	38
State	61	16	26	7	11	11	18	27	44
Local	61	15	25	4	7	8	13	34	56

TABLE C-5
RESPONDENTS' MEMBERSHIP IN RELIGIOUS ORGANIZATIONS

Religious Organization	Number	Not a Member		Attend Regularly		Attend Infrequently		Never Attend	
		N	%	N	%	N	%	N	%
Church	105	12	11	54	51	30	29	9	9
Cursillista	104	93	89	7	7	3	3	1	1
Guadalupanas	104	95	91	6	6	1	1	2	2

TABLE C-6

RESPONDENTS' HIERARCHY OF POLITICAL INVOLVEMENT
IN CHICANO RELATED ACTIVITIES

Activity	Number	Yes		No	
		N	%	N	%
Gladiatorial					
Held office	93	0	0	93	100
Candidate	93	0	0	93	100
Gone to demonstration	84	9	11	75	89
Gone to rally	87	16	18	71	82
Fund raising	93	8	9	85	91
Attended caucus	92	20	22	72	78
Active party member	90	17	19	73	81
Transitional					
Gone to meeting	91	23	25	68	74
Contacted official	86	13	15	73	85
Spectator					
Worn button .	82	18	22	64	78
Influenced others	82	28	34	54	66
Initiated discussion	82	35	43	47	57
Voted	86	30	35	56	65
Wrote letter	85	4	5	81	95

TABLE C-7

RESPONDENTS' HIERARCHY OF POLITICAL INVOLVEMENT
IN OLD-AGE RELATED ACTIVITIES

Activity	Number	Yes		No	
		N	%	N	%
Gladiatorial					
Held Office	92	1	2	91	99
Candidate	92	2	2	90	98
Gone to demonstration	85	4	5	81	95
Gone to rally	83	4	5	79	95
Fund raising	92	4	4	88	96
Attended caucus	92	9	10	83	90
Active party member	90	12	13	78	87
Transitional					
Gone to meeting	86	10	12	76	88
Contacted official	82	5	6	77	94
Spectator					
Worn button	83	7	8	76	92
Influenced others	84	20	24	64	76
Initiated discussion	83	16	19	67	81
Voted	83	7	8	76	92
Wrote letter	83	3	4	80	96

TABLE C-8

RESPONDENTS' HIERARCHY OF POLITICAL INVOLVEMENT
IN GENERAL CITIZENSHIP ACTIVITIES

Activity	Number	Yes		No	
		N	%	N	%
Gladiatorial					
Held office	96	0	0	96	100
Candidate	96	0	0	96	100
Gone to demonstration	88	4	5	84	95
Gone to rally	90	7	8	83	92
Fund raising	96	4	4	92	96
Attended caucus	95	13	14	82	86
Active party member	92	14	15	78	85
Transitional					
Gone to meeting	90	12	13	78	87
Contacted official	90	14	16	76	84
Spectator					
Worn button	82	19	23	63	77
Influenced others	86	43	50	43	50
Initiated discussion	86	51	59	35	41
Voted	91	52	57	39	43
Wrote letter	87	8	9	79	91

APPENDIX D

ATTITUDES

This appendix describes political attitudes of the
Hispanic elderly according to seven categories. In
analyzing responses with respect to these areas, the
categories are useful in examining the various
attitudes expressed about nonparticipation by older
Hispanics. With few exceptions, the categories are
also used for the questions asked throughout Chapters
III and IV.

1. Negative role expectations. The female does
not participate because she is too busy being a mother
and wife and thus her role does not permit it; the
older person is too busy with the family and church;
they were raised differently from the youth of today,
and thus it is not appropriate for older persons to be
involved in politics and organizations.

2. Fear and distrust. The older persons are
afraid they may somehow be adversely affected by
political participation, perhaps even to the extent of
loss of Social Security and citizenship and
deportation. They fear discrimination, are distrustful
of leaders and politics, feel that they will be "used,"
and dislike politics and its "infighting."

3. Generational and ideological conflicts. The
older person feels that Hispanic political leaders,
activists, and organizations cannot be trusted, that
self-interest predominates on the part of the younger
Hispanic, and that the younger Hispanic does not
respect older persons. The older person may also feel
that the younger Hispanic is too assimilated, does not
know Spanish, or cannot communicate properly with the
older Hispanic. This category includes a dislike and
fear of the Hispanic movement, disagreement with its
ideology, and a dislike of its militancy. For example,
the older person feels that the Hispanic is too
disorganized in his approach to politics and is not
dealing with the issues directly related to the
well-being of the older Hispanic. He also feels that
the younger Hispanic does not care about the older
person.

4. Negative self-image and apathy. Older
Hispanics with this attitude do not participate in
politics because they feel too old and useless,

195

apathetic ("just don't care") or fatalistic ("I'm just planning to die"). They are not interested in politics or feel that no one cares about their contribution.

5. <u>Functional</u> <u>capability</u>. In this attitude, political inactivity is attributed to poor health or a lack of transportation.

6. <u>Illiteracy</u>. Here the failure to participate in politics is attributed to lack of education or an inability to speak English.

7. <u>Communication</u>. The older Hispanic feels that he is uninformed about the activities and goals of the political movement because no one has made an effort to contact him. He sometimes feels there has not been enough effort made to organize older people. There is also a lack of understanding of why Hispanics have to be involved in politics.

In addition to categorizing attitudes about nonparticipation, categories about why older persons should participate were established.

1. <u>Social</u> <u>activities</u>. This is the attitude that older persons should participate for recreation, mutual self-help, or to meet friends.

2. <u>Community</u> <u>activities</u>. Older Hispanics feel that they should participate in order to be united and organized. They should participate in community and political activities.

3. <u>Nonsegregation</u>. This attitude is characterized as a belief that Hispanics should not participate in social and community activities solely on an ethnic basis but should work with and become involved with White and Black elderly.

4. <u>Advocacy</u>. This is the feeling that advocacy is needed, either with others or through the older person's own efforts.

5. <u>Hispanic</u> <u>movement</u>. The older person believes that the Hispanic movement and Hispanic politics benefit everyone, and thus the older persons should also participate.

BIBLIOGRAPHY

Acuna, R. Occupied America: A History of Chicanos.
2nd Edition. New York: Harper and Row, 1981.

Agger, R., and Goldrich, D. "Community Power Structures
and Partisanship." American Sociological Review 23
(August 1958): 383-392.

Agger, R., and Ostrom, V. "Political Participation in a
Small Community." In Political Behavior, pp.
138-148. Edited by H. Eulau, S. Eldersveld, and M.
Janowitz. Glencoe, Ill.: The Free Press, 1956.

Agger, R.; Goldrich, D.; and Swanson, B. The Ruler and
The Ruled: Political Power and Impotence in
American Communities. New York: Wiley, 1964.

The Aging Population of Santa Clara County: A Study.
San Jose, Calif.: Social Planning Council of Santa
Clara County, 1973.

Aguayo, J.M. "Latinos: Los Que Importan Son Ustedes."
Sales and Marketing Management, July 11, 1977, p.
26.

Allan, G. "Illegal Aliens." American Opinion, January
1978, p.39.

Almond, G. "Comparative Political Systems." Journal of
Politics 18 (1956): 391-409.

Almond, G., and Verba, S. The Civic Culture.
Princeton, N.J.: Princeton University Press,
1963.

Alvarez, J. "A Demographic Profile of Mexican
Immigration to the United States, 1910-1950."
Journal of Inter-American Studies 38 (July 1966):
471-496.

Anderson, J. E. Public Policy-Making. 2nd Edition.
New York: Holt Reinhart and Winston, 1979.

Anson, R. "Future Research Techniques and Resources:
Applications for Hispanos." La Luz, May 1978,
p.32.

Banfield, E. The Moral Basis of a Backward Society.
Glencoe, Ill.: The Free Press, 1958.

197

Bechill, W. "Politics of Aging and Ethnicity." In Ethnicity and Aging, pp. 137-147. Edited by D.E. Gelfeld and A.J. Kutzik. New York: Springer Publishing, 1979.

Bell,D.; Kasschau, P.; and Zellman, G. Delivering Services to Elderly Members of Minority Groups: A Critical Review of the Literature. Santa Monica: Rand Corporation, 1976.

Bengtson, V.L.; Cuellar, J.; and Ragan, P. "Stratum Contrasts and Similarities in Attitudes Toward Death." Journal of Gerontology 32 (1977): 76-88.

Berelson, B.; Lazarsfeld, P. F.; and McPhee, W. Voting. Chicago: University of Chicago Press, 1954.

Binstock, R. "Interest-Group Liberalism and the Politics of Aging." The Gerontologist 12 (1972): 265-280.

Binstock, R. "Aging and the Future of American Politics." Annals of the American Academy of Political and Social Sciences 415 (September 1974): 199-212.

Brown; Rosen; Hill; and Olivas. The Condition of Education for Hispanic Americans. Washington, D.C.: National Center for Education Statistics, 1980.

Buchanon, W. "An Inquiry into Purposive Voting." Journal of Politics 18 (May 1956): 281-296.

Butler, D., and Stokes, D. Political Change in Britain. New York: St. Martin's Press, 1971.

Campbell, A. "The Passive Citizen." Acta Sociologia. fasc. 1-2 (1962): 14.

Campbell, A. "Politics through the Life Cycle." The Gerontologist 2, no. 2 (Summer 1971): Part I, 112-117.

Campbell, A.; Converse, P.; Miller, W.; and Stokes, D. The American Voter. New York: Wiley, 1960.

Campbell, A.; Gurin, G.; and Miller, W. The Voter Decides. Evanston, Ill.: Row, Peterson, 1954.

Campbell, A., and Kahn, R. The People Elect a President. Ann Arbor: University of Michigan, Survey Research Center, 1952.

Campbell, J., and Strate, J. "Are Old People Conservative?" The Gerontologist. 21 (1981): 580-591.

Carp, F. Factors in Utilization of Services by the Mexican American Elderly. Palo Alto: American Institute for Research, 1968.

Conway, M., and Feigert, F. Political Analysis. Boston: Allyn and Bacon, 1972.

Cottrell, W.F. "Government Functions and the Politics of Age." In Handbook of Social Gerontology. pp. 624-665. Edited by C. Tibbitts. Chicago: University of Chicago Press, 1960.

Cottrell, W. F. Government and Non-Government Organizations. 1971 White House Conference on Aging. Washington, D.C.: Government Printing Office, 1971.

Crittenden, J. "Aging and Political Participation." Western Political Quarterly 16 (1963): 323-331.

Crouch, B. M. "Aging and Institutional Support: Perceptions of Older Mexican-Americans." Journal of Gerontology 27 (1972):524-529.

Cuellar, J.B. "The Senior Citizen's Club: The Older Mexican-American in the Voluntary Association." In Life's Career: Aging, pp. 207-230. Edited by B. Myerhoff, and A. Simic. Beverly Hills, CA: Sage Publications, 1978.

Cuellar, J.B. and Weeks, J. Minority Elderly Americans: The Assessment of Needs and Equitable Receipt of Public Benefits as a Prototype for Area Agencies on Aging. Final Report. San Diego, CA: Allied Home Health Association, October 1980.

Cutler, N. "Political Characteristics of Elderly Cohorts in the Twenty-First Century." In Aging: Social Change, pp. 127-157. Edited by S.B. Kiesler. New York: Academic Press, 1981.

Dahl, R. Who Governs? Democracy and Power in an American City. New Haven: Yale University Press, 1961.

Davies, J. Human Nature in Politics: The Dynamics of Political Behavior. New York: Wiley, 1963.

Derbyshire, R. "Children's Perceptions of the Police: A Comparative Study of Attitudes and Attitude Change." In Chicanos: Social and Psychological Perspectives. Edited by N. Wagner and M. Haug. St. Louis: C.V. Mosby, 1971.

Dieppa, A. Retirement: A Comparative Study of Mexican Americans and Anglos. Ph.D. Dissertation. Denver University, 1977.

Donahue, W., and Tibbitts, C. Politics of Age. Ann Arbor: University of Michigan Press, 1962.

Doherty, R. P. "Mexican Americans: Growing Old in the Barrio." In Employment Prospects of Aged Blacks, Chicanos, & Indians. Washington, D.C.: National Council on Aging, 1971.

Duaree, J. Feasibility Study of the Needs of the Spanish-Speaking Elderly in an Urban Setting. Los Angeles: East Los Angeles Health Task Force, 1975.

Eribes, R.A., and Rawls, M.B. "The Underutilization of Nursing Home Facilities by Mexican American Elderly in the Southwest." The Gerontologist. 18 (1978): 363-371.

Estes, C. The Aging Enterprise. San Francisco: Jossey-Bass, Inc.: 1979.

Fairchild, H. Dictionary of Sociology. Ames, Iowa: Adams, 1944.

Federal Council on Aging. Policy Issues Affecting the Minority Elderly. Washington D.C.: Government Printing Office, 1980.

Friis, H. "Issues in Social Security Politics in Denmark." In Social Security In International Perspective, pp. 129-150. Edited by S. Jenkins. New York: Columbia University Press, 1969.

Fuchs, L. Hawaii Pomo: A Social History. New York: Harcourt, Brace, and World, 1961.

Fuchs, L. American Ethnic Politics. New York: Harper and Row, 1968.

Galarza, E.; Gallegos, H.; and Samora, J. Mexican-Americans in the Southwest. Santa Barbara, CA: McNelly and Loftin, 1970.

Gallo, P. Ethnic Alienation. Rutherford, N.J.: Fairleigh Dickinson University Press, 1974.

Gans, H. The Urban Villagers. Glencoe, Ill.: The Free Press, 1962.

Garcia, C., ed. Chicano Politics. New York: MSS Information Corp., 1973.

Garcia, C., ed. La Causa Politica. Notre Dame: University of Notre Dame, 1974.

Gibson, G. "El Centro del Barrio."A Progress Report. San Antonio Texas: Our Lady of the Lake College, 1973. (Mimeographed.)

Glade, W., and Anderson, C. The Political Economy of Mexico. Madison: University of Wisconsin Press, 1963.

Glenn, N. "Aging , Disengagement, and Opinionation." Public Opinion Quarterly 33 (1969): 17-33.

Glenn, N. "Aging and Conservatism." Annals of the American Academy of Political and Social Sciences 415 (1974): 176-186.

Glenn, N., and Grimes, M. "Aging, Voting, and Political Interest." American Sociological Review 33 (1968): 563-575.

Gordon, M. Assimilation in American Life. New York: Oxford University Press, 1964.

Grebler, L.; Moore, J.; and Guzman, R. The Mexican American People. New York: The Free Press, 1970.

Grindley, W. and Hentzell, S. California Hispanics--A Report from the Near Horizon Symposia. Menlo Park, Ca.: SRI International, 1981.

Gross, R.; Gross, B.; and Seidman, S., eds. The New Old: Struggling for Decent Aging. Garden City, N.Y.: Anchor Press/Doubleday, 1978.

Guttman, D. Perspective on Equitable Share in Public Benefits by Minority Elderly. Executive Summary. Washington D.C.: The Catholic University Of America, 1980.

Hausknecht, M. The Joiners. New York: Bedminister Press, 1962.

Havighurst, R.G. "A Report of a Special Committee of the Gerontological Society." The Gerontologist 11, no. 4 (Winter 1971): Part II.

Heller, C. Mexican-American Youth. New York: Random House, 1966.

Hernandez, A. and Mendoza, J., eds. The National Conference on the Spanish-speaking Elderly. Kansas City: National Chicano Social Planning Council, 1975.

Hill, A. A Study of Michigan's Chicano Population. Ann Arbor: Institute of Gerontology, University of Michigan, 1971.

Holmes, J. Politics in New Mexico. Albuquerque: University of New Mexico Press, 1967.

Holtzman, A. "Analysis of Old Age Politics in the United States." Journal of Gerontology. 9 (1954): 56-66.

Holtzman, A. The Townsend Movement: A Political Study. New York: Bookman Associates, 1963.

Hudson, R.B. and Binstock, R.H. "Political Systems and Aging." In Handbook of Aging and the Social Sciences, pp. 369-400. Edited by R.H. Binstock, and E. Shanas. New York: D. Van Norstand Company, 1976.

Hudson, R.B. The Aging in Politics: Process and Policy. Springfield, Ill.: Charles C. Thomas, 1981.

Jensen, J. "Political Participation: A Survey in Evanston, Illinois." A Master's thesis, Northwestern University, 1960.

Lane, R. Political Life. Glencoe. Ill.: The Free Press, 1959.

Lazarsfeld, P. F.; Berelson, B.; and Gaudet, H. The People's Choice. New York: Duell, Sloan, and Pearce, 1944.

Leonard, O.E. and Johnson, H. W. Low Income Families in the Spanish-Surname Population of the Southwest. U.S. Department of Agriculture, Economic Research Service. Washington, D.C.: Government Printing Office, 1967.

Leonard, O.E. "The Rural Spanish-Speaking People of the Southwest." In Older Rural Americans,. pp. 239-261. Edited by E.G. Youmans. Lexington: University of Kentucky Press, 1967.

Levy, M. "A Philosopher's Stone." World Politics. 5 (July 1953):555-568.

Litwak, E., and Szeleny, I. "Different Primary Group Structures and Their Functions." School of Social Work, University of Michigan, 1968. (Mimeographed.)

Lopata, H.A. "Social Relations of Widows in Black and White Urban Communities." Administration on Aging publication No. 25. U.S. Department of Health, Education, and Welfare, limited circulation, N.D.

Luevano, R. "Attitudes of Elderly Mexican Americans Toward Nursing Homes in Stanislaus County." Paper Presented at the 9th Annual Conference on the National Association of Chicano Studies. Riverside, Ca., April 2-4, 1981.

Marcias, R.F. "U.S. Hispanics in 2000 A.D.- Projecting the Number." Agenda Magazine. 11(1977): 16.

Maldonado, D. "The Chicano Aged." Social Work. 20 (1975): 213-216.

Maslow, A. Motivation and Personality. New York: Harper and Row, 1954.

Matthiessen, P. _Sal Si Puedes._ New York: Random House, 1969.

McCleskey, C., and Merrill, B. "Mexican American Political Behavior in Texas." _Social Science Quarterly._ 53(March 1973): 784-798.

Mendenhall, W.; Ott, L.; and Schaffer, R. _Elementary Survey Sampling._ Belmont, Ca.: Wadsworth, 1971.

"Mexican American." _Business Week._ May 29, 1971.

Milbrath, L. _Political Participation._ Chicago: Rand McNally, 1965.

Miranda, M. "Latin American Culture and American Society: Contrasts." In _The National Conference on the Spanish Speaking Elderly._ pp. 43-46. Edited by A. Hernandez and J. Mendoza. Kansas City: National Chicano Social Planning Council, 1975.

Moore, J.W. _Mexican American._ Englewood Cliffs, N. J.: Prentice-Hall, 1970.

Moore, J.W. "Situational Factors Affecting Minority Aging." _The Gerontologist._ 11, no. 1 (1971): Part 2, 88-93.

Morales, A. "Chicano-Police Riots." In _Chicano: Social and Psychological Perspectives._ pp. 184-202. Edited by N. Wagner and M. Haug. St Louis: C.V. Mosby, 1971.

Newquist, D.; Berger, M.; Kahn, K.; Martinez, C.; and Burton, L. _Prescription for Neglect: Experiences of Older Blacks and Mexican Americans with the American Health System._ Andrus Gerontology Center, University of Southern California, 1979.

Newton, F., and Ruiz, R. "Chicano Culture and Mental Health among the Elderly." In _Chicano Aging and Mental Health_, pp. 38-75. Edited by M. Miranda and R.A. Ruiz. Washington D.C.: Government Printing Office, 1981.

Nie, N.; Bent, D.; and Hill, H. _Statistical Package for the Social Sciences_ (_SPSS_). New York: McGraw-Hill, 1970.

Nie, N.; Verbas, S.; and Kim, J. "Political Participation and the Life Cycle." Comparative Politics 6 (1974): 319-340.

Novak, M. "Why Latin America is Poor." The Atlantic Monthly, March 1982, pp. 66-75.

Olson, M. "Social Participation and Voter Turnout: A Multivariate Analysis." American Sociological Review 37 (1972): 317-333.

Owens, Y.; Torres-Gil, F.; and Wolf, R. "The Minority Elderly and the Conference." In 1971 White House Conference on Aging: An Overview of the Conference Process. Edited by James Schulz. The Florence Heller Graduate School For Advanced Studies In Social Welfare, Brandeis University, February 1973.

Pachon, H. "Recurring Issues in Hispanic Political Participation." Perspectives on the U.S. Hispanic Population and its Political Participation. NALEO Education Fund. 1(January 1982): 5-7.

Paz, O. The Labyrinth of Solitude. New York: Grove Press, 1961.

Pinner, F. A.; Jacobs, P.; and Selznick, P. Old Age and Political Behavior. Berkeley: University of California Press, 1959.

Pratt, H.J. "Old Age Associations In National Politics." Annals of the American Academy of Political and Social Science. 415 (1974): 106-119.

Pratt, H.J. The Gray Lobby. Chicago: The University of Chicago Press, 1976.

Purcell, J.F. "Mexican Social Issues." In Mexico-United States Relations. Proceedings of the Academy of Political Science. 34 (1981) 43-54.

Putnam, J.K. Old Age Politics in California: From Richardson to Reagan. Stanford, Ca.: Stanford University Press, 1970.

Pye, L., and Verba, S., eds. Political Culture and Political Development. Princeton, N. J.: Princeton University Press, 1965.

Riley, M.W. and Foner, A. Aging and Society. Vol. I. New York: Russell Sage Foundation, 1968.

Riley, M.; Johnson, M.; and Foner, A. Aging and Society. Vol III. New York: Russell Sage Foundation, 1973.

Robinson, J.; Rusk, J.; and Head, K. Measure of Political Attitudes. Ann Arbor: Survey Research Center, University of Michigan, 1968.

Rose, A. "The Subculture of the Aging." In Middle Age and Aging. Edited by B. Neugarten. Chicago: University of Chicago Press, 1968.

Rowan, H. "A Minority Nobody Knows." In Chicano Politics, pp. 8-20. Edited by C. Garcia. New York: MSS Information Corporation, 1973.

Rubenstein, D. "The Social Participation of the Black Elderly." Ph.D. Dissertation. The Florence Heller Graduate School For The Advanced Studies in Social Welfare, Brandeis University, 1971.

Samuelson, R. "Benefit Programs for the Elderly--Off Limits to Federal Budget Cutters?" National Journal October 3, 1981, pp. 1757-1762.

Sandoval, R. and Martinez, D. "Police Brutality-The New Epidemic." Agenda. September/October 1978.

Santa Clara County Transportation Study. Final Report. San Jose: Office of the County Executive, Santa Clara County, Ca., 1969.

Scott, R. "Mexico: The Established Revolution." In Political Culture and Political Development, pp. 330-395. Edited by S. Verba and L. Pye. Princeton, N. J.: Princeton University Press, 1965.

Searing, D.; Schwartz, J.; and Lind, A. "The Structuring Principle: Political Socialization and Belief Systems." American Political Science Review 67, no. 2 (1973): 415-432.

Sellitz, C.; Jahoda, M.; Deutsch, M.; and Cook, S. Research Methods in Social Relations. New York: Holt, Reinhart and Winston, 1959.

Shuttles, G. _Social Order in the Slum_. Chicago: University of Chicago Press, 1968.

Simic, A., and Myerhoff, B., eds. _Life's Career:Aging_ Beverly Hills: Sage Publishing. 1978.

Solis, F. "Cultural Factors in Programming of Services for Spanish-speaking Elderly." In _The National Conference on the Spanish-speaking Elderly_. Edited by A. Hernandez and J. Mendoza. Kansas City:National Chicano Social Planning Council, 1975.

Sotomayor, M. "A Study of Chicano Grandparents in an Urban Barrio." A D.S.W. Dissertation. University of Denver, 1973.

Sotomayor, M. "Social Change and the Spanish-speaking Elderly." In _National Conference on the Spanish-speaking Elderly_, pp. 26-29. Edited By Hernandez, A. and Mendoza, J. Kansas City: National Chicano Social Planning Council, 1975.

Steiner, S. _La Raza: The Mexican American_. New York: Harper and Row, 1969.

Tingsten, H. _Political Behavior: Studies in Election Statistics_. London: P. S. King, 1937.

Torres-Gil, F. "Los Ancianos de la Raza: A Beginning Framework for Research, Analysis, and Policy." A Master's Thesis, The Florence Heller Graduate School For Advanced Studies In Social Welfare, Brandeis University, 1972.

Torres-Gil, F.; Newquist, D.; and Simonin, M. _Transportation: The Diverse Aged_. Washington, D.C.: Government Printing Office, May, 1976.

Torres-Gil, F. "Concerns of the Spanish-speaking Elderly." In _Minority Aging: Second Institute on Minority Aging Proceedings_, pp. 2-7. Edited by E.P. Stanford. San Diego: Center on Aging, San Diego State University, 1975.

Torres-Gil, F. and Becerra, R. "The Politcal Behavior of the Mexican American Elderly." _The Gerontologist_. 17, no. 5 (1977): 392-399.

Torres-Gil, F.; Newquist, D.; and Simonin, M. "Housing: The Diverse Aged." Project M.A.S.P. (Minority Aging and Social Policy). Andrus Gerontology Center, University of Southern California, 1978.

Torres-Gil, F. "Age, Health, and Culture: An Examination of Health Among Spanish Speaking Elderly." In Hispanic Families, pp. 83-102. Edited by M. Montiel. The National Coalition of Hispanic Mental Health and Human Services Organizations (COSSHMO), 1978.

Torres-Gil, F. and Negm, M. "Policy Issues Concerning the Hispanic Elderly." Aging, nos. 305-306 (March-April 1980): 2-5.

Torres-Gil, F. "The Political Potential of the Hispanic Elderly." In Perspectives on the U.S. Hispanics Population and its Political Participation. NALEO Education Fund, 1, no. 4, (1982): 4-5.

Trela, J. "Some Political Consequences of Senior Center and Other Old Age Group Memberships." The Gerontologist 11, no. 2 (Summer 1971): 118-123.

Trela, J. "Age Structure of Voluntary Associations and Political Self-Interest among the Aged." Sociological Quarterly 13 (1972): 118-123.

Trela, J. "Old Age and Collective Political Action." Paper Presented at the National Gerontological Society, San Juan, Puerto Rico, 1973.

Ulibarri, H. "Teacher Awareness of Socio-Cultural Difference in Multi-Cultural Classrooms." Sociology and Social Research 45 (October 1960): 52-68.

U. S. Congress, Senate Special Committee on Aging. Availability and Usefulness of Federal Programs and Services to Elderly Mexican-Americans. Parts 1-5. Washington DC.: Government Printing Office, 1970.

U.S. Department of Commerce, Bureau of the Census. Current Population Reports. P-20, No. 143, 1965, 1969, 1970. Washington D.C.: Government Printing Office, 1971.

U.S. Department of Commerce, Bureau of the Census. Current Population Report. Persons of Spanish Origin in the United States: March 1979. Issued October 1980.

U.S. Department of Commerce, Bureau of the Census. Supplementary Reports. Age, Sex, Race, and Spanish origin of the population by regions, divisions and states: 1980. May 1981. (a)

U.S. Department of Commerce, Bureau of the Census. Current Population Reports: Population Characteristics. Voting and Registration in the Election of November 1980 (Advance Report). Issued January 1981. (b)

U.S. Department of Health, Education and Welfare. Toward a National Policy on Aging. Vol. I and II. Proceedings of the 1971 White House Conference on Aging, November 28-December 2, 1971. Final Report. Washington, D.C.: Government Printing Office, 1972.

U.S. Department of Health and Human Services, Human Development Services, Administration on Aging. Statistical Reports on Older Americans Characteristics of the Hispanic Elderly, May 1981.

U.S. Department of Labor. Handbook of Labor Statistics. Washington, D.C.: Government Printing Office, 1975.

Valdes, D. "A Political History of New Mexico." Denver, Colorado; revised, 1971. (Mimeographed.)

Valle, R. "Amistad-Compadrazgo as an Indigenous Webwork Compared with the Mental Health Network." Ph.D. Dissertation, University of Southern California, Los Angeles, 1974.

Valle, R. and Mendoza, L. The Elderly Latino. Center on Aging, San Diego State University. San Diego: The Campanile Press, 1978.

Valle, R. and Martinez, C. "Natural Networks of Elderly Latinos of Mexican Heritage: Implications for Mental Health." In Chicano Aging and Mental Health, pp. 76-117. Edited by M. Miranda and R. A. Ruiz. National Institute of Mental Health. Washington D.C.: Government Printing Office, 1981.

Velez, C. "The Aged and the Political Process." In Institute on Aging: An Orientation for Mexican-American Community Workers in the Field of Aging, pp. 10-13. Edited by A. Hernandez and J. Mendoza. Kansas City: National Chicano Social Planning Council, 1973.

Velez, C.R.; Verdugo, R.; and Nunez, F. "Politics and Mental Health Among Elderly Mexicanos." In Chicano Aging and Mental Health, pp. 118-155. Edited by M. Miranda and R. A. Ruiz. National Institute of Mental Health. U. S, Department of Health and Human Services. Washington D.C.: Government Printing Office, 1981.

Verba, S. Comparative Political Culture." In Political Culture and Political Development, pp. 512-560. Edited by L. Pye, and S. Verba. Princeton, N. J.: Princeton University Press, 1965.

Verba, S. and Nie, N. Participation in America. New York: Harper and Row, 1972.

Ward, R. "Japan: The Continuity of Modernization." In Political Culture and Political Development, pp. 27-82. Edited by L. Pye and S. Verba. Princeton, N. J.: Princeton University Press, 1965.

Welch, S.; Comer,J.; and Steinman, J. "Political Participation Among Mexican-Americans: An Exploratory Examination." Social Science Quarterly. 53 (March 1973): 799-813.

Woodward, J. and Roper, E. "Political Activity of American Citizens." American Political Science Review 44 (1950): 872-885.

Yinger, M. "Anomie, Alienation, and Political Behavior." In Handbook of Political Psychology, page numbers. Edited By J. Knutson. San Francisco: Jossey-Bass, 1973.

ABOUT THE AUTHOR

Fernando M. Torres-Gil, Ph.D. is an Assistant Professor of Gerontology and Public Administration at the Leonard Davis School of Gerontology of the University of Southern California. Dr. Torres-Gil received his undergraduate degree in Political Science in 1970 from San Jose State University and an MSW in 1972 and Ph.D. in 1976 in Social Policy, Planning and Research from the Florence Heller Graduate School for Advanced Studies in Social Welfare at Brandeis University. Before joining the faculty of USC, he held several appointments in government, including special Assistant to Joe Califano, former Secretary of Health, Education and Welfare; and Special Assistant to Patricia R. Harris, former Secretary of Health and Human Services. He has received numerous awards and honors, including a HUD Urban Studies Fellowship, a Presidential appointment to the Federal Council on Aging from 1978 to 1982 and selection as a White House Fellow. In addition, he is active in many organizations and on many boards. He was a founder of the National Hispanic Council on Aging and the California Statewide Association on Hispanic Aging. He was a member of the American Bar Association's Commission on Legal Problems of the Elderly from 1979 to 1982 and a delegate to the 1981 White House Conference on Aging. A member of both the Western and National Gerontological Societies, Dr. Torres-Gil is a national expert in gerontology, ethnicity and social policy. His numerous publications include Transportation: The Diverse Aged, with Deborah Newquist & Mary Simonin (U.S. Government Printing Office, 1976); "Age, Health and Culture: An Examination of Health Among Spanish Speaking Elderly" in Hispanic Families (ed. M. Montiel, COSSMHO, 1978); and "Political Behavior of Mexican-American Elderly," with Rosina Becerra in the Gerontologist (October, 1977).

DATE

AUG. 31. 1991